Rainbow Edition

Reading Mastery III
Workbook A

Siegfried Engelmann • Susan Hanner

Macmillan/McGraw–Hill

Columbus, Ohio

SRA Macmillan/McGraw-Hill
250 Old Wilson Bridge Road
Suite 310
Worthington, Ohio 43085
Printed in the United States of America.
ISBN 0-02-686391-X
1 2 3 4 5 6 7 8 9 0 DBH 99 98 97 96 95 94

LESSON A

A

Story items

Fill in the blanks.

☐ **1.** Name three insects. _ant_ _fit_ _butterfly_

☒ **2.** How many parts does the body of an insect have? _three_

☐ **3.** How many parts does the body of an ant have? _three_

☐ **4.** Is a spider an insect? _no_

☐ **5.** All insects have _six_ legs.

☐ **6.** Name three animals that have six legs. _ant_ _butterfly grasshopper_

☒ **7.** How many legs do spiders have? _eight legs_

☒ **8.** How many parts does a spider's body have? _two_

Skill items

9. | If a cup has spots, it is hot. |

Circle every cup that is hot.

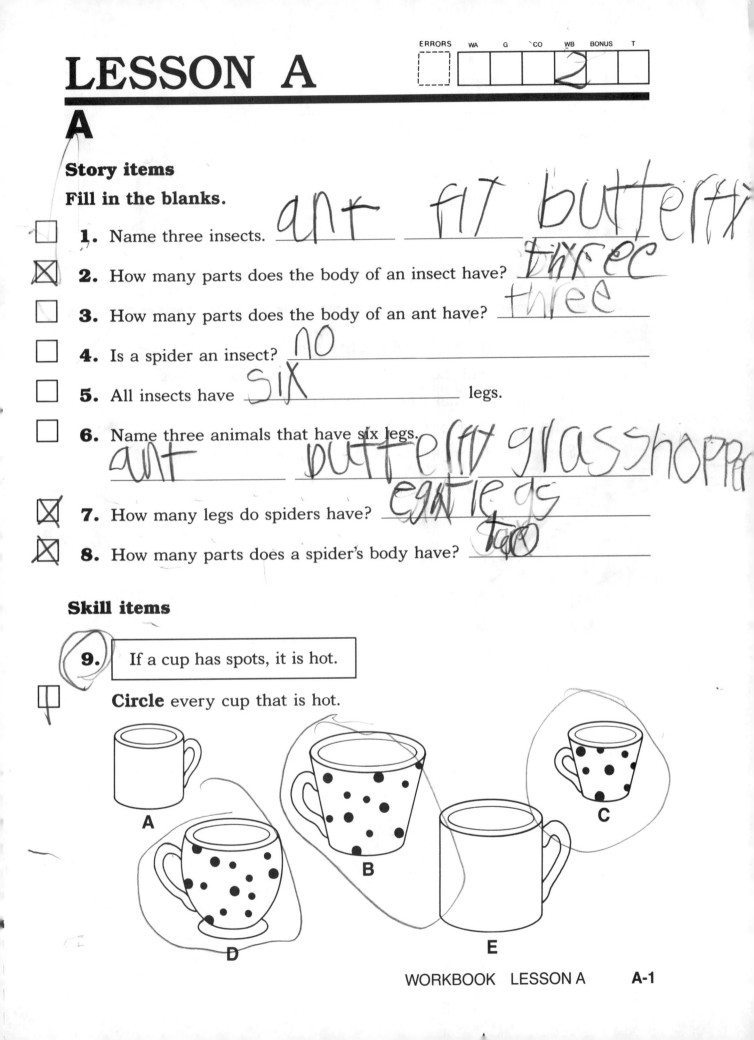

10. Find out who has frogs.

> Rule: There are frogs in every tin cup.

Ellen has a tin cup.

Tim does not have a tin cup.

Sid has a tin cup,

Who has frogs? _Sid_ _Eleen_

B

Rules for Reading Checkouts

- You must read the starred part in one minute or less.
- Students who make no reading errors get 7 points.
- Students who make 1, 2, or 3 errors get 3 points.
- Students who make more than 3 errors get no points.

LESSON B

A

Story items

Fill in the blanks.

☐ **1.** What do all living things need? _Water_

☐ **2.** What do all living things make? _babies_

ok ☒ **3.** What else do all living things do? _grow_

☐ **4. a.** Is a fly a living thing? _Yes_

ok ☒ **b.** Name two things you know about a fly. _grow_
need water

☐ **5. a.** Is a dog a living thing? _Yes_

☐ **b.** So you know that a dog needs _water_.

ok ☒ **c.** And you know that a dog _grow water_.

☐ **6. a.** Is a chair a living thing? _No_

ok ☒ **b.** Does a chair need water? _No_

Skill items

7. | Every big box has kittens in it. |

ok ☒ **Cross out** every box with kittens in it.

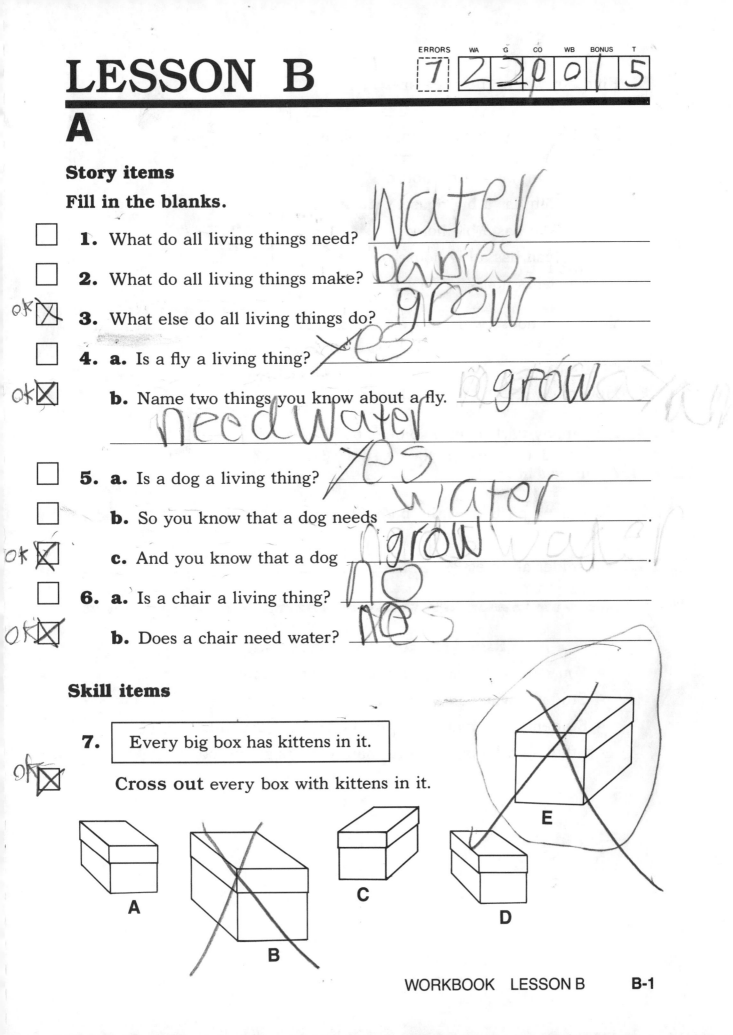

8. Find out where the mice are.

> Rule: Every big house has mice in it.

Tom has a little house.
Bob has a big house.
Ann has a big horse.
Jean has a big house.
Sam's house is very big.

☐ Who has a house with mice? _Jean Sam Bob_

Review items

☒ **9.** How many legs do spiders have? _Eght_

☒ **10.** How many parts does a spider's body have? _four_

☐ **11.** All insects have _six_ legs.

☐ **12.** How many parts does the body of an insect have? _three_

☐ **13.** Is a spider an insect? _no_

B

Rules for Reading Checkouts

- You must read the starred part in one minute or less.
- Students who make no reading errors get 7 points.
- Students who make 1, 2, or 3 errors get 3 points.
- Students who make more than 3 errors get no points.

LESSON C

A

Story items

Fill in the blanks.

1. All trees have _roots_

2. How many things do a tree's roots do? _two_

3. Roots keep the tree from _falling down_.

4. Roots carry _water_ to the tree.

5. Could trees live if they didn't have roots? _no_

6. Do trees begin to grow **in the winter** or **in the spring**?
the spring

7. Trees begin to grow when their roots get _warm_.
warmer

8. Look at these trees.

a. **Circle** the tree that has deeper roots.

b. **Make a box around** the tree that begins to grow first every year.

9. **Fill in each box** with the right word.

ground   roots   water

A | water

B | root

C | ground

Skill items

10.

| If a boy is tall, he has a brother. |

Circle every boy who has a brother.

A   B   C   D   E   F

11. Find out who is smart.

> Rule: The people with hats are smart.

Kim has a hat.

Pete has a hat.

Tom does not have a hat.

Jane has a hat.

Ron does not have a hat.

☐ Who is smart? _____ *Kim Pete Jane*

Review items

12. You know that:

☐   **a.** Living things need _____ *water* .

☒   **b.** Living things make _____ *babies* .

☒   **c.** Living things also _____ *grow* .

☐ **13.** All insects have __*6*_____ legs.

☒ **14.** How many parts does the body of an insect have? __*3*____

☒ **15.** Cats are living things. Name 3 things you know about cats.

_____ *cat needs water* _____

_____ *grow make babies* _____

_____

B

Rules for Reading Checkouts

- You must read the starred part in one minute or less.
- Students who make no reading errors get 7 points.
- Students who make 1, 2, or 3 errors get 3 points.
- Students who make more than 3 errors get no points.

LESSON D

A

Story items

Fill in the blanks.

☒ **1.** Which boy wanted red walls? ___Tims brother___

☒ **2.** Which boy wanted white walls? ___Tim___

☒ **3.** Which boy said, "Let's have striped walls?" ___Tim___

☐ **4. a.** After the boys agreed to have striped walls, they went to a ___paint store___.

☐ **b.** Did they talk to a man or a woman? ___a women___

☒ **c.** Tim said, "We want ___strip___ paint."

Skill items

5. | If it is fat and has 4 legs, it is a ronk. |

☐ **Make a line under** every ronk.

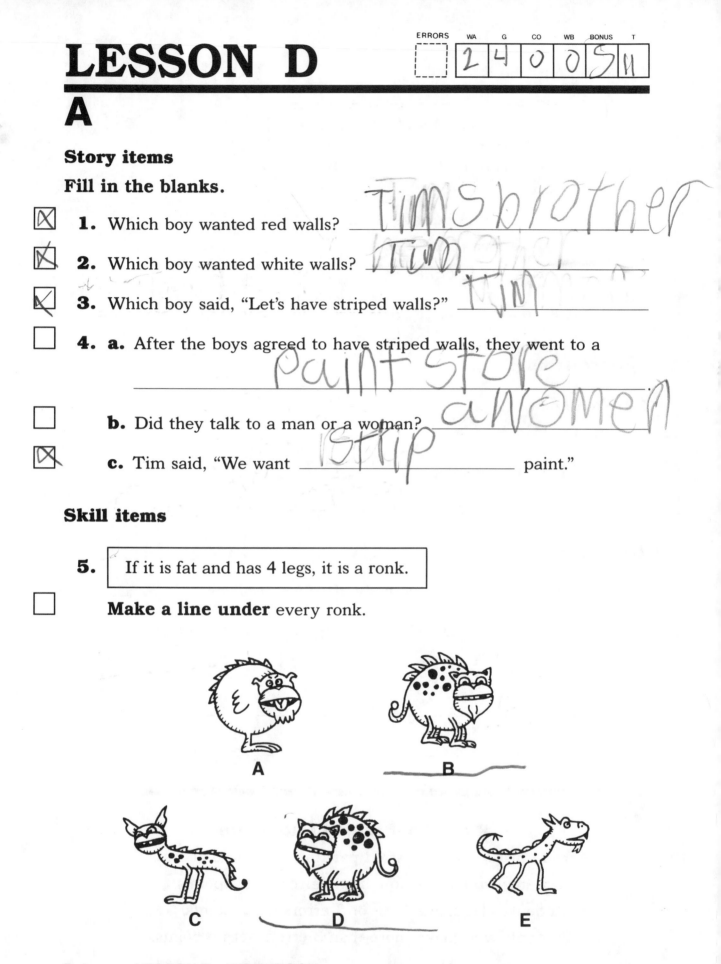

A   B

C   D   E

6. Find out who has a bug.

> Rule: Every fat bottle has a bug in it.

    Pat's bottle is fat.

    Fred's bottle is not fat.

    Don's bottle is fat.

    Nick's bottle is not fat.

    Jan's bottle is not fat.

Who has a bug? _____ Pat's Don's _____

Review items

7. Look at these trees.

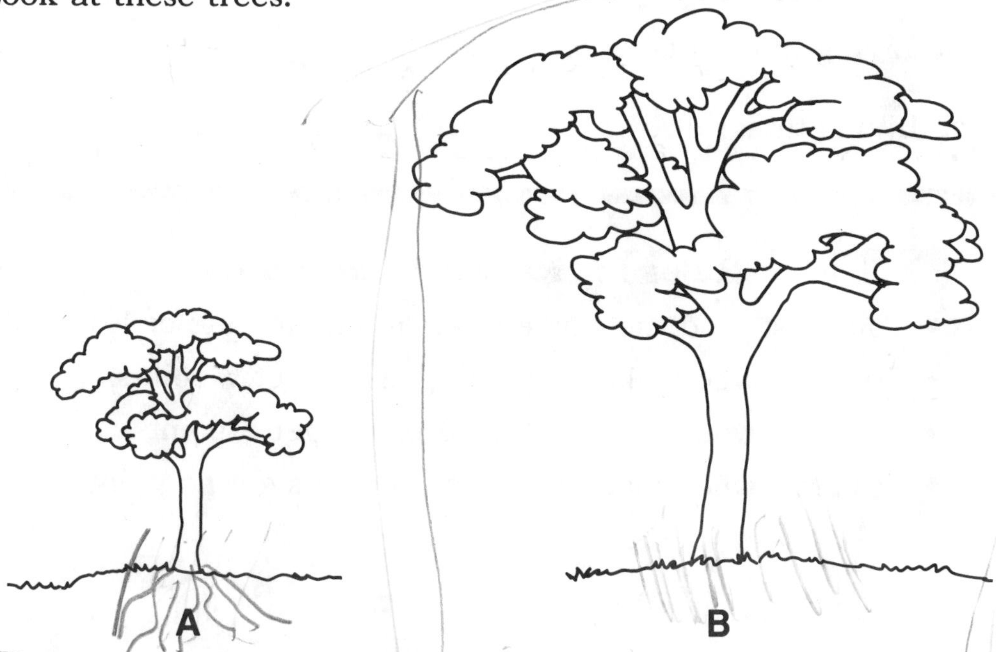

A   B

    a. Make a line under the tree that begins to grow first every year.

    b. Make a box around the tree that has deeper roots.

8. Do trees begin to grow **in the winter** or **in the spring?**

spring _____

☒ **9.** Name 2 things that a tree's roots do.

carry water

help the tree stand up

☒ **10.** How many parts does a spider's body have? *two*

☒ **11.** How many legs do spiders have? *eight*

☒ **12.** How many parts does the body of an insect have? *three*

☒ **13.** All insects have *six* legs.

14. You know that:

☐ **a.** Living things need *water*.

☒ **b.** Living things make *babies*.

☒ **c.** Living things also *grow*.

B

Rules for Reading Checkouts

- You must read the starred part in one minute or less.
- Students who make no reading errors get 7 points.
- Students who make 1, 2, or 3 errors get 3 points.
- Students who make more than 3 errors get no points.

LESSON 1

A

5/5 = 100%

A✓

In today's lesson, you read the names for some things. Use what you learned to do this item.

1. Under each picture, write what the picture shows. The names are in the box.

apples	grapes	shirt	pets	~~frog~~
playing football	cutting hair	fish	~~log~~	~~fish~~
~~canoe~~	~~field~~	fishing pole	bell	~~tiger~~

☐ **a.** canoe

☐ **b.** frog

☐ **c.** Tiger

☐ **d.** field

☐ **e.** log

WORKBOOK   LESSON 1   1

B

Story items

☐ **2.** What's the title of the story? **Circle the answer.**
- The Tiger and the Dog
- The Tiger and the Frog *(circled)*
- The Dog and the Frog

☐ **3.** Name two pets that Tom's brother had.
① Frog and the mean ② tiger

☐ **4.** Did Tom open the right box? ___ No ___

5. Finish the rule that Tom's brother told Tom. "I keep the frog in the box that is off."

6. Use the rule and see which box has a frog in it.

☐ **a.** What do you know about the striped box? ___ That the frog is inside ___

☐ **b.** Is this box striped? ___ yes ___

☐ **c.** So does the rule tell that there's a frog in this box? ___ yes ___

A

☐ **d.** Is this box striped? ___ no ___

☐ **e.** So does the rule tell that there is a frog in this box? ___ no ___

B

☐ **f.** Use the rule and **underline** the box that has a frog in it.

C   **D**   **E**   **F**

Skill items

7. Here are titles for different stories.

- Jane Goes on a Train
- My Dog Likes Cats
- The Hot Summer
- The Best Meal

☐ **a.** One story tells about eating good food. What's the title of that story? _the best meal_

☐ **b.** One story tells about somebody taking a trip. What's the title of that story? _Jane goes on a Train_

☐ **c.** One story tells about a time of year when people go swimming a lot. What's the title of that story? _the hot summer_

☐ **d.** One story tells about pets. What's the title of that story? _My dog likes cats_

LESSON 2

ERRORS	WA	G	WB	BONUS	T
☐	2	4	2	2	

8

_2 + 4 + 2 + 2 =_

my dog likes cats

A

In today's lesson, you read about things people eat. Use what you learned to do these items.

1. Use the rule and see which things are good for you.

☐ **a.** What do you know about sweet things like apples and grapes? _They are good for you_

☐ **b.** Is this a sweet thing like an apple or a grape? _Yes_

orange
A

☐ **c.** So is this sweet thing good for you? _yes_

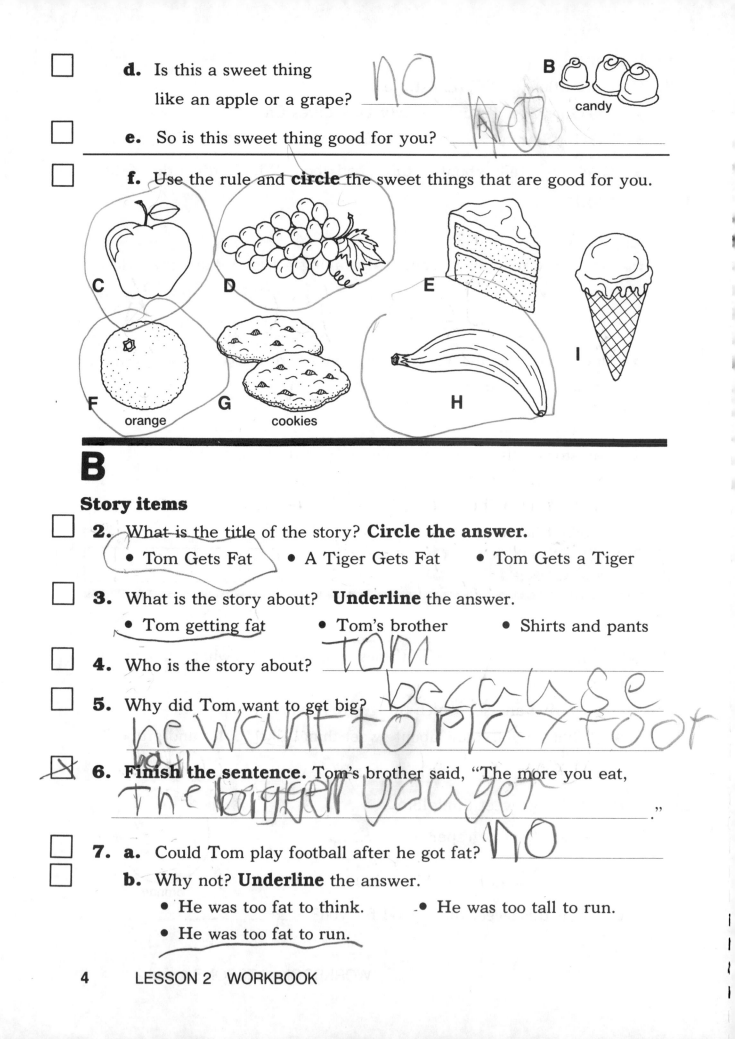

d. Is this a sweet thing like an apple or a grape? _no_

e. So is this sweet thing good for you? _____

f. Use the rule and **circle** the sweet things that are good for you.

C   D   E

F orange   G cookies   H   I

candy

B

Story items

2. What is the title of the story? **Circle the answer.**

- Tom Gets Fat   • A Tiger Gets Fat   • Tom Gets a Tiger

3. What is the story about? **Underline** the answer.

- Tom getting fat   • Tom's brother   • Shirts and pants

4. Who is the story about? _Tom_

5. Why did Tom want to get big? _because he want to play football_

6. **Finish the sentence.** Tom's brother said, "The more you eat, _the bigger you get no_ ."

7. a. Could Tom play football after he got fat? _No_

b. Why not? **Underline** the answer.

- He was too fat to think.   • He was too tall to run.

- He was too fat to run.

8. Name two things that Tom ate.

① *Cake and* ② _____

Hot dog

9. Picture A shows Tom **before** he ate and ate and ate. One of the other pictures shows Tom **after** he ate and ate and ate. **Cross out** that picture.

A   B   C   D

Skill items

10. You're going to circle the right objects. Here's the rule:

There is a dog behind every striped door.

  a. What do you know about every striped door?

The strip door has a dog behind it. no

  b. Is this object a striped door? ____ *no*

  c. So does the rule tell that there

     is a dog behind this object? ____ *no*

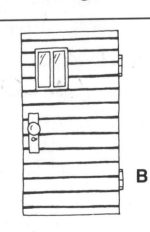

A

  d. Is this object a striped door?

Yes

  e. So does the rule tell that there is a dog

     behind this object? *Yes*

B

f. Use the rule and **circle** each object that you **know** has a dog behind it.

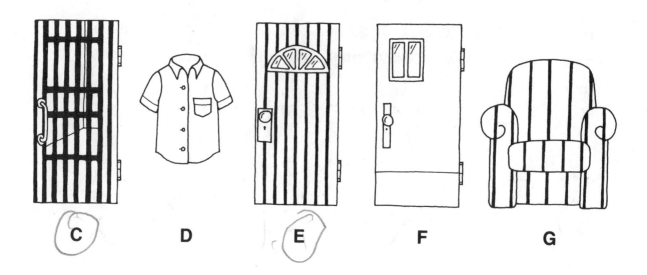

C   D   E   F   G

11. Find out who ate ice cream. Here's the rule:

Every little boy ate ice cream.

Pete is a little boy.   Sam is a little boy.

Fred is not a little boy.   Bob is not a little boy.

Mike is a little boy.

Who ate ice cream? _Sam Pete and Mike_

12. Here are titles for different stories:

- The Red Bike   • How to Bake a Cake   • Three Fat Rats

a. One story tells about making something to eat. What's the title of that story?

How to Bake

b. One story tells about some animals that eat too much. What's the title of that story?

Three Fat Rat

c. One story tells about a toy. What's the title of that story?

The Red Bike a

LESSON 3

A

In today's lesson, you read about make-believe animals. Use what you learned to do this item.

☐ **1. Circle** the pictures of animals that are make-believe.

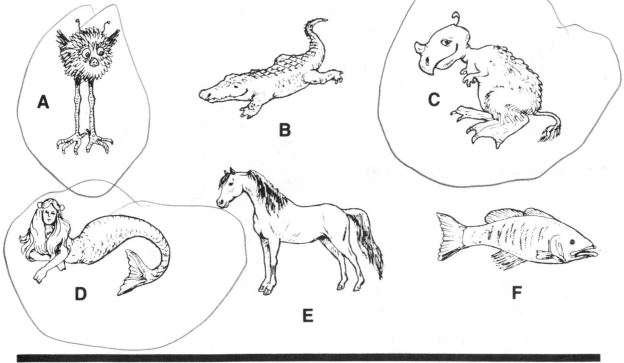

B

Story items

☐ **2.** What is the title of the story? **Underline the answer.**

- Moops Find Bob and Don
- Bob and Don Find Moops
- Bob and Don Find Mops

☐ **3. Finish the sentence.** The wise old man said, "The more you cut its

hair, _The faster it's hair grows_ ."

☐ **4.** Who did not listen to the wise old man? _bob_

☐ **5.** What happened to the moop's hair when Bob cut it?

grow biger and biger

WORKBOOK   LESSON 3   7

6. Did Bob have fun with his moop? _____ *no*

7. Are moops **real** or **make-believe**? _____ *believe*

8. a. One of the pictures shows Don's moop in a room.
   Circle that picture.

   b. One of the pictures shows Bob's moop in a room.
   Cross out that picture.

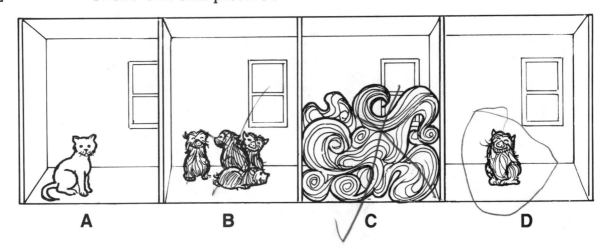

A   B   C   D

Skill items

9. Find out who has a moop that eats glass. Here's the rule:

All mean moops eat glass.

   Jean's moop is mean.

   Meg's moop is mean.

   Fran's moop is not mean.

   Jack's moop is not mean.

   Tom's moop is not mean.

   Who has a moop that eats glass? _____ *Jean meg*

10. You're going to underline Tim's frogs. Here's the rule:

Tim's frogs are spotted.

   a. What do you know about Tim's frogs? *spotted*

   b. Is this frog spotted? _____ *no*

   c. So is this one of Tim's frogs? _____ *no*

A

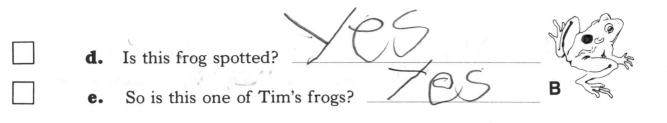

d. Is this frog spotted? _____Yes_____

e. So is this one of Tim's frogs? _____Yes_____ **B**

f. Use the rule and **underline** Tim's frogs.

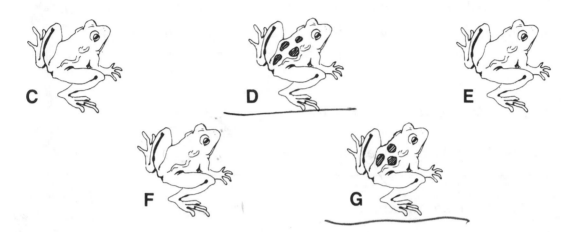

C   D   E

F   G

11. Here are titles for different stories:

- Liz Goes to the Zoo
- A Pretty New Hat
- The Green Dog

a. One story tells about someone who went to look at animals. What's the title of that story?

_____Liz goes to the zoo_____

b. One story tells about a funny-looking animal. What's the title of that story?

_____The green dog_____

c. One story tells about something you put on your head. What's the title of that story?

_____a pretty new Hat_____

LESSON 4

A

In today's lesson, you read about forests. Use what you learned to do these items.

1. Use the rule and see which trees grew in a forest.

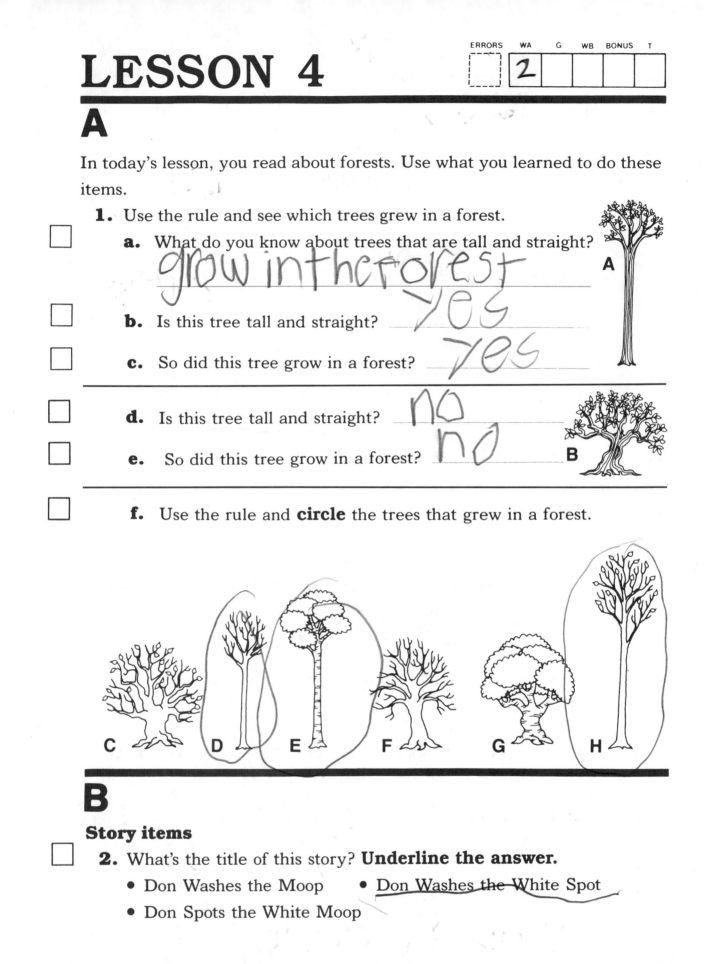

☐   a. What do you know about trees that are tall and straight?
        grow in the forest

☐   b. Is this tree tall and straight? *yes*

☐   c. So did this tree grow in a forest? *yes*

☐   d. Is this tree tall and straight? *no*

☐   e. So did this tree grow in a forest? *no*

☐   f. Use the rule and **circle** the trees that grew in a forest.

C   D   E   F   G   H

B

Story items

☐   2. What's the title of this story? **Underline the answer.**
    • Don Washes the Moop   • <u>Don Washes the White Spot</u>
    • Don Spots the White Moop

10   LESSON 4   WORKBOOK

3. Did Don like white coats? _____ no _____

4. Finish the sentence. The old man said, "The more you wash this

spot, _The bigger it will get._ "

5. What color was the coat that the old man gave Don? _gray_

6. What happened to the spot when Don washed it? _It got bigger_

_____

7. What color was the coat after Don washed it? _white_

8. Circle the picture that shows a forest.

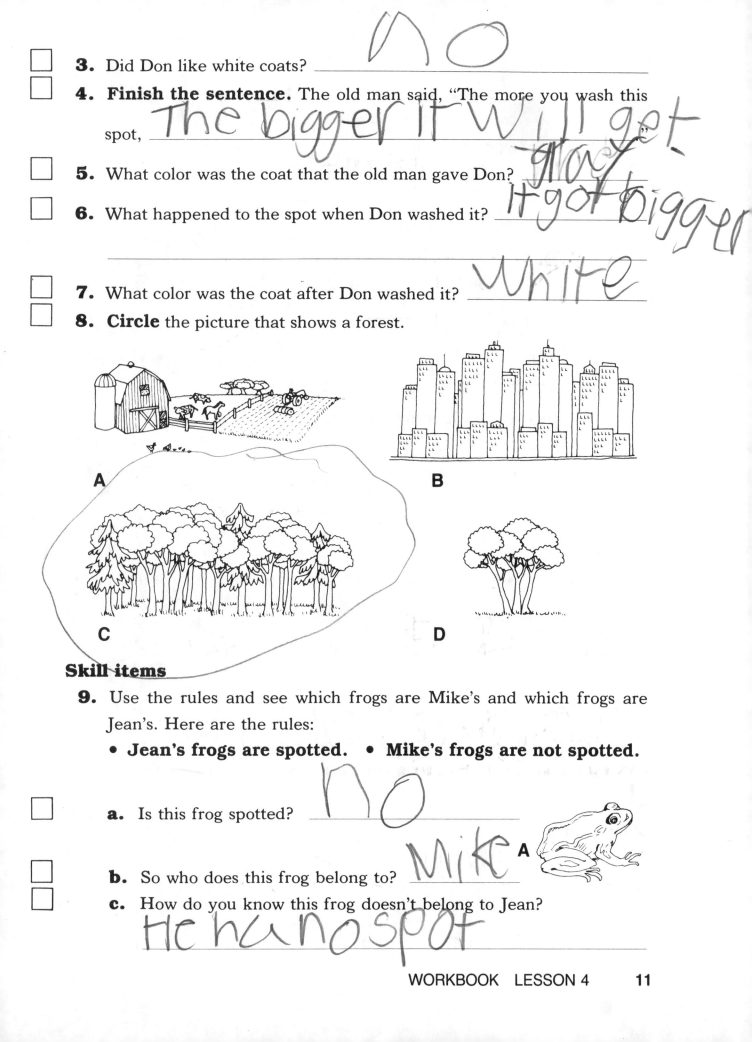

A

B

C

D

Skill items

9. Use the rules and see which frogs are Mike's and which frogs are Jean's. Here are the rules:

> • **Jean's frogs are spotted.** • **Mike's frogs are not spotted.**

a. Is this frog spotted? _no_

b. So who does this frog belong to? _Mike_   A

c. How do you know this frog doesn't belong to Jean?

He has no spot

d. Is this frog spotted? _yes_

e. So who does this frog belong to? _Jean_

f. How do you know this frog doesn't belong to Mike?

it ha spots

g. **Make a box around** Jean's frogs.

h. **Underline** Mike's frogs.

10. Find out which dogs just ate a cake. Here's the rule:

Every sitting dog just ate a cake.

A black dog is sitting.

A brown dog is lying down.

A white dog is standing.

A spotted dog is running.

A gray dog is sitting.

Which dogs just ate a cake? _a whit dog_

Review items

11. Write the word **make-believe** under every make-believe animal.

A _make belieue_   B _make believe_   C

12. **Circle** the sweet things that are good for you.

A orange

F orange

B

G

C

D

H

E

I candy

LESSON 5

A

Story items

1. **Finish the rule** that the old man told Don. "Do not cut down any

   trees from the _fields._

   Cut trees from the _forest._"

2. Did Don know what a forest is? _no_

3. Did Don cut down the right trees? _no_

4. Use the rule and see which logs came from field trees.

   a. What do you know about logs that are not tall and straight?
   short,

   b. Is this log tall and straight? _yes no_

   c. So did this log come from a field tree? _no_   **A**

   d. **Cross out** the logs that came from field trees.

   B   C   D   E   F   G   H

Skill items

5. You're going to cross out the right objects. Here's the rule:

   Every box has a dollar in it.

   a. What do you know about every box?
   every box has a dollar in it

b. Is this object a box? _____no_____

A

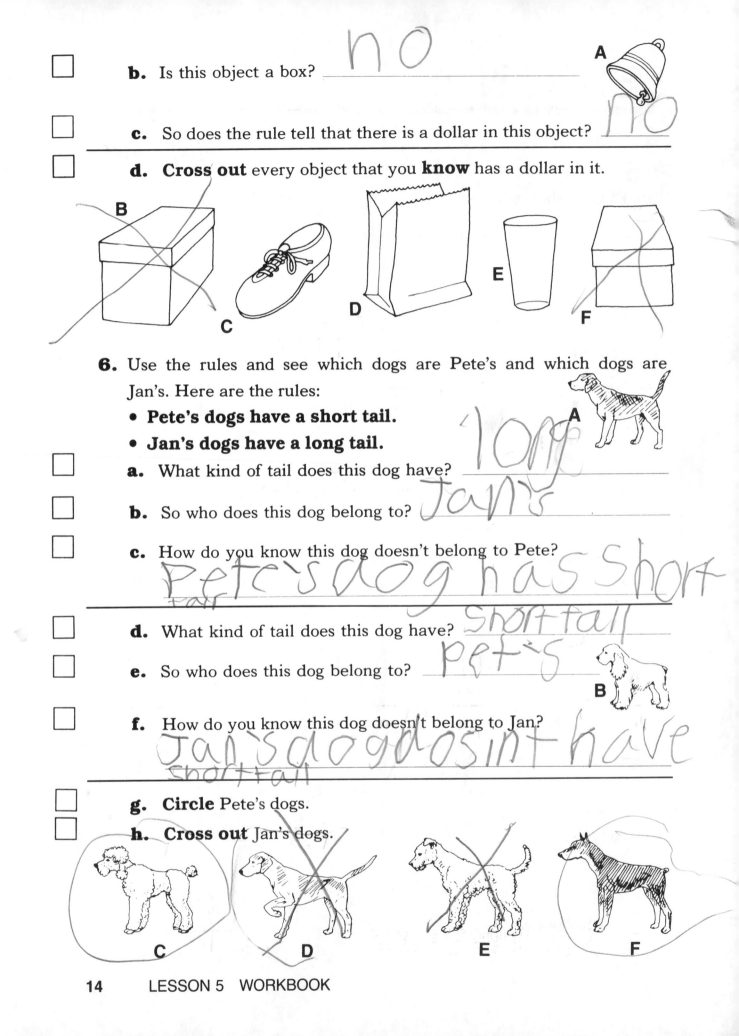

c. So does the rule tell that there is a dollar in this object? _____no_____

d. Cross out every object that you **know** has a dollar in it.

B

C

D

E

F

6. Use the rules and see which dogs are Pete's and which dogs are Jan's. Here are the rules:

- **Pete's dogs have a short tail.**
- **Jan's dogs have a long tail.**

a. What kind of tail does this dog have? _____long_____

A

b. So who does this dog belong to? _____Jan's_____

c. How do you know this dog doesn't belong to Pete? _____Pete's dog has short tail_____

d. What kind of tail does this dog have? _____short tail_____

e. So who does this dog belong to? _____pet's_____

B

f. How do you know this dog doesn't belong to Jan? _____Jan's dog dosint have short tail_____

g. Circle Pete's dogs.

h. Cross out Jan's dogs.

C

D

E

F

Review items

7. Write the word **make-believe** under every make-believe animal.

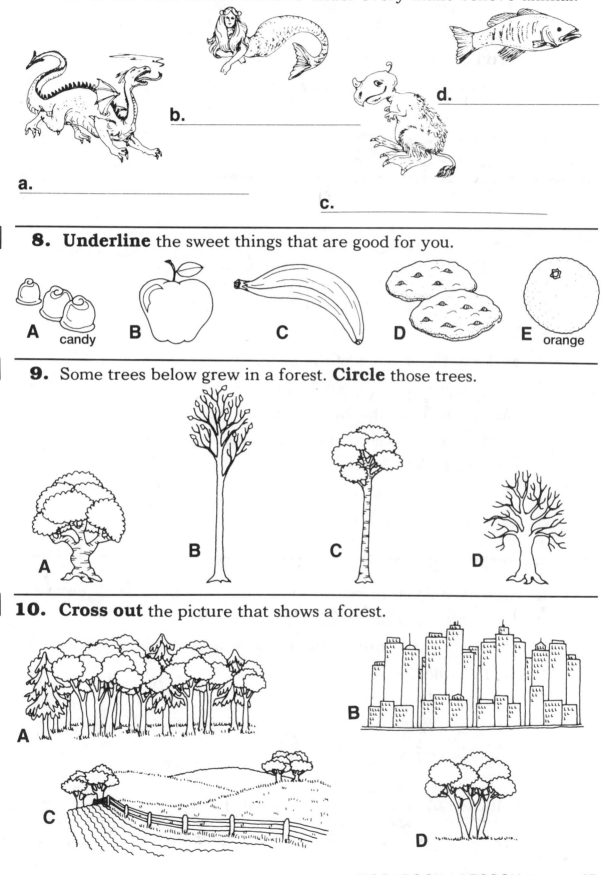

a. _____

b. _____

c. _____

d. _____

8. **Underline** the sweet things that are good for you.

A candy   B   C   D   E orange

9. Some trees below grew in a forest. **Circle** those trees.

A   B   C   D

10. **Cross out** the picture that shows a forest.

A   B   C   D

B

Rules for Reading Checkouts

- You must read the starred part in one minute or less.
- Students who make no reading errors get 7 points.
- Students who make 1 or 2 errors get 3 points.
- Students who make more than 2 errors get no points.

ERRORS	WA	G	WB	BONUS	T

LESSON 6

A

Story items

☐ 1. **Finish the sentence.** A canoe is a small _bout_____.

☐ 2. **Fill in the blank.** You use a _paddle_____ to make a canoe move.

3. **a.** Look at the picture.

☐   **Make a T** at the **top** of the paddle to show where one hand would grab the paddle.

☐   **b. Make an M** in the **middle** of the paddle to show where the other hand would grab the paddle.

☐ 4. **a.** Look at the picture below. Make an arrow **over each canoe** to show which way the canoe is moving.

☐   **b.** Make an arrow **under each paddle** to show which way the paddle is moving in the water.

A   B   C

☐ 5. **Finish the rule** about the waves a canoe makes. The faster a canoe moves, _The waves will get bigger_____.

6. Use the rule and see which canoe is moving very fast and which canoe is not moving at all.

a. What do bigger waves tell you? *canoe is moving fast*

b. Is this canoe making **big waves**, **little waves**, or **no waves?** *big waves*

A

c. So how is this canoe moving — fast or slow or not at all? *canoe is fast*

d. How do you know that this canoe is moving fast? *because the waves are big*

e. Is this canoe making **big waves**, **little waves**, or **no waves?** *little waves*

f. So how is this canoe moving — fast or slow or not at all? *slow moving*

B

g. How do you know that this canoe is not moving fast? *the waves are little*

h. One canoe below is moving very fast. Write the letter of that canoe. *E*

i. One canoe below is not moving at all. Write the letter of that canoe. *D*

C D E

Skill items

7. You're going to see which bugs are Pete's and which bugs are Ann's.

Here are the rules:

- **Pete's bugs have six legs.**
- **Ann's bugs have eight legs.**

☐   **a.** How many legs does this bug have? ___eight legs___

☐   **b.** So who does this bug belong to? ___Ann___

☐   **c.** How do you know this bug does not belong to Pete?

it has eight legs

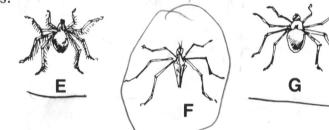

☐   **d.** How many legs does this bug have? *it has six legs*

☐   **e.** So who does this bug belong to? ___Pet___

☐   **f.** How do you know this bug doesn't belong to Ann?

because it doesn't have eight legs

☐   **g.** **Circle** Pete's bugs.

☐   **h.** **Underline** Ann's bugs.

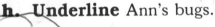

Review items

☐   **8.** Write the word **make-believe** under each make-believe animal.

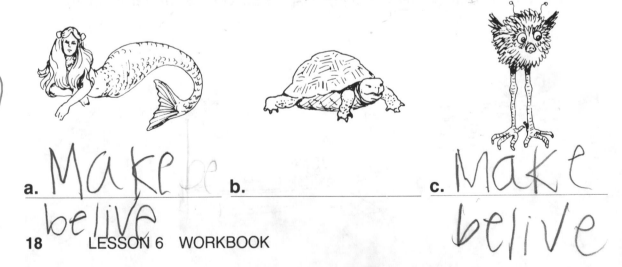

a. *Make believe*   **b.** _____   **c.** *make believe*

9. **Make a box around** the picture that shows a forest.

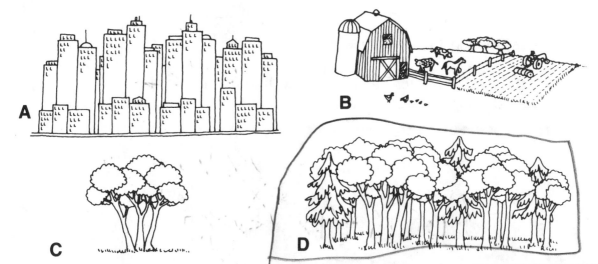

A B C D

10. Some of the logs below were cut from field trees. **Cross out** those logs.

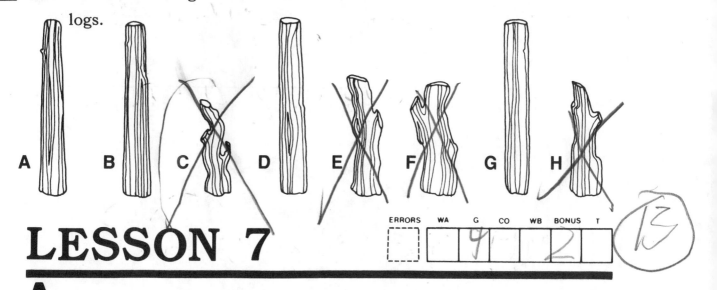

A B C D E F G H

LESSON 7

ERRORS	WA	G	CO	WB	BONUS	T
		4			2	

A

Story items

1. Name two kinds of canoes that Indians made.

① canoes from bark ② dugout canoes

2. Did **all** Indians make canoes? no

3. **Fill in the blank.** Indians made bark canoes from the bark of

birch _____ trees.

4. What would happen to a bark canoe if it didn't have a frame?

fall appert _____

5. Use the rule and see which logs would make good dugout canoes.

☐   **a.** Is this log tall and straight? _yes_

☐   **b.** So would this log make a good dugout canoe? _yes_   **A**

☐   **c. Cross out** all the logs that would make good dugout canoes.

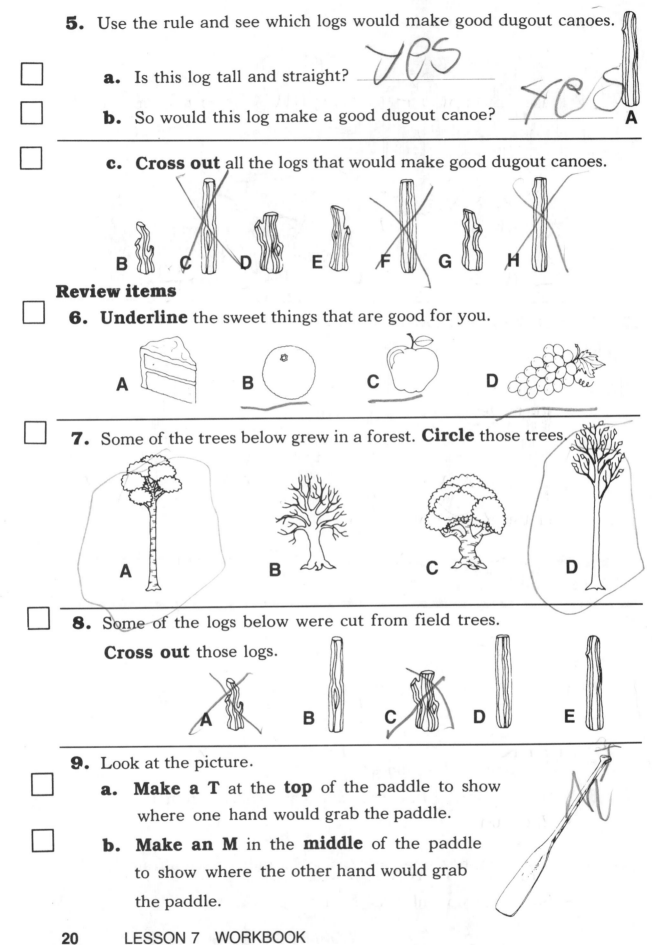

B   C   D   E   F   G   H

Review items

☐   **6. Underline** the sweet things that are good for you.

A   B   C   D

☐   **7.** Some of the trees below grew in a forest. **Circle** those trees.

A   B   C   D

☐   **8.** Some of the logs below were cut from field trees.

Cross out those logs.

A   B   C   D   E

9. Look at the picture.

☐   **a. Make a T** at the **top** of the paddle to show where one hand would grab the paddle.

☐   **b. Make an M** in the **middle** of the paddle to show where the other hand would grab the paddle.

10. Look at the picture below.

   a. Make an arrow **over each canoe** to show which way the canoe is moving.

   b. Make an arrow **under each paddle** to show which way the paddle is moving in the water.

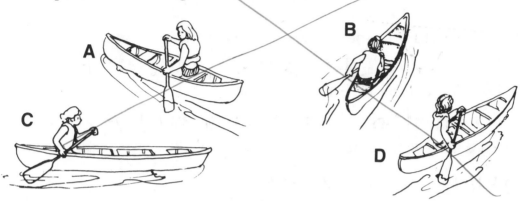

A   B   C   D

---

11. a. **Finish the rule** about the waves a canoe makes. The faster a canoe moves, *TheBiggerThewaves get* _____.

   b. Look at the picture below. One canoe is moving very fast. Write the letter of that canoe. *A* _____

   c. One canoe is not moving at all. Write the letter of that canoe *C*

A   B   C

B

Rules for Reading Checkouts

   • You must read the starred part in one minute or less.
   • Students who make no reading errors get 7 points.
   • Students who make 1 or 2 errors get 3 points.
   • Students who make more than 2 errors get no points.

LESSON 8

A

Story items

1. Who is this story about? _Don_

2. What's the title of the story? **Underline the answer.**
   - <u>Don Makes the Fish Too Hungry</u>
   - Don Makes a Canoe
   - Don Makes the Fish Eat a Canoe

3. How many fish did Don get before he rang the bell? _____

4. **Finish the sentence.** The old man said, "The more you ring this bell, _The Hunger The Fish_"

5. Don rang the bell many times to make the fish very, very hungry. How many times did he ring it? **Circle the answer.**
   - 10
   - (50)
   - 100

6. Look at the picture below.

   a. Which letter is in the middle of the lake? _____

   b. Which letter is on the shore of the lake? _____

   c. Which letter is in the forest? _____

   d. Which letter is on the path? _____

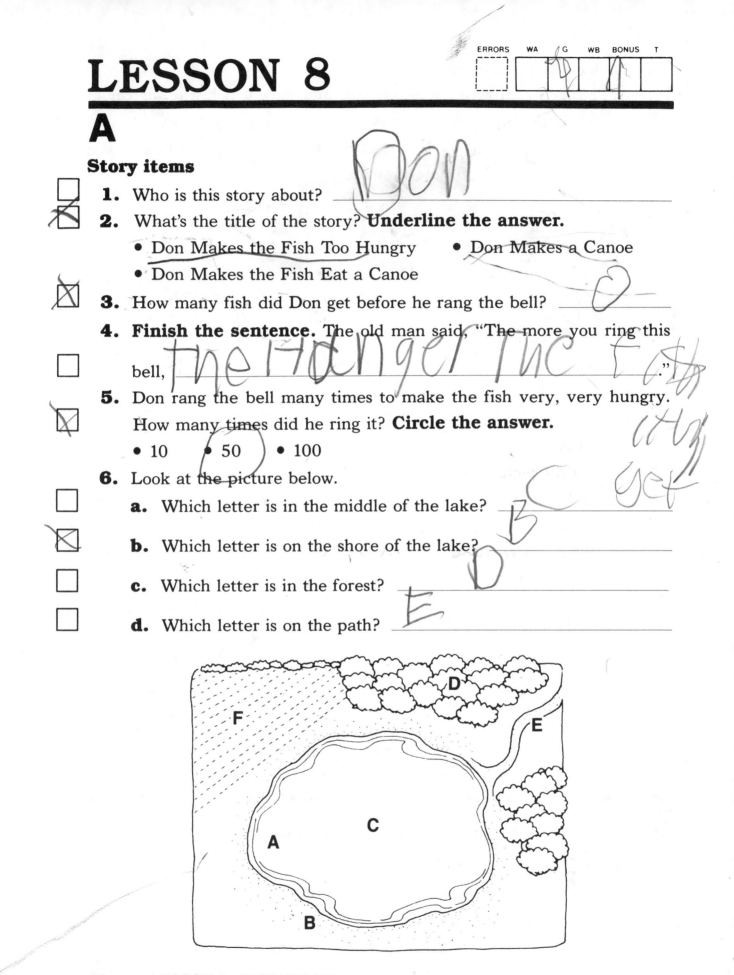

7. The picture below shows how many times each bell rang.

    a. **Circle** the picture that shows when the fish will eat the most.

    b. **Cross out** the picture that shows when the fish will eat the least.

A   B   C   D   E

Skill items

8. Here's the rule: **If you find it in the mud, it is wet.**

    a. You find trobes in the mud. So what else do you know about

    trobes? _____

    b. You find blookers in the mud. So what else do you know about

    blookers? _____

Review items

9. Look at the picture below.

    a. Make an arrow **over each canoe** to show which way the canoe is moving.

    b. Make an arrow **under each paddle** to show which way the paddle is moving in the water.

A   B   C   D

10. Name two kinds of canoes that Indians made.

   ①_____ ②_____

11. Some trees below grew in a forest. **Underline** those trees.

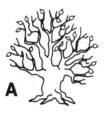  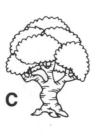 

A   B   C   D

LESSON 9

A

In today's lesson, you read about water lilies. Use what you learned to do these items.

1. What's the name of pretty flowers that grow in the water?

   water lilies

2. Name two colors that water lilies can be.

   ① *Pink and* ② *yellow*

B

Story items

3. What was wrong with the canoe that Jane used?

   it has now in it

4. The old man told Jane a rule about the canoe. **Finish the rule.** "If you sit near the back, *The canow won sink* "

5. What tool did Jane use to make the canoe move across the lake?

   padle

6. Find the **X** on the map. **Draw a line from the X** to show the short cut Jane took.

   CREEP

7. As Jane went across the lake, something got stuck to the front of the canoe.

   a. What got stuck? _water lilies_

   b. Did Jane want it? _Yes_

   c. Why didn't she try to get it? _the canoe will sink_

8. Did Jane remember the rule about the canoe? _Yes_

9. Here's the canoe that Jane used.

   a. **Put an X** where Jane sat.

   b. **Make a Y** where the lily got stuck.

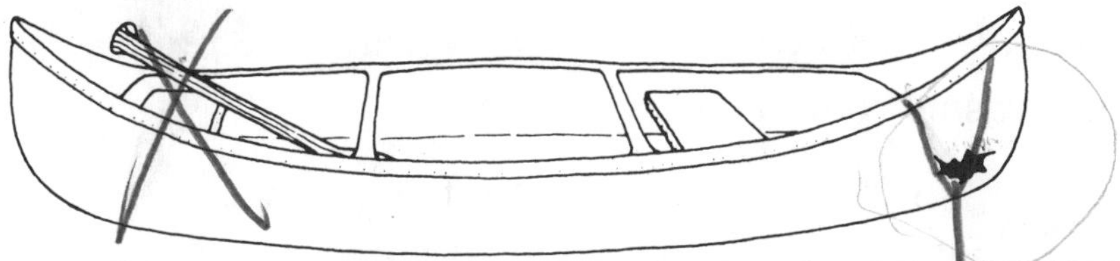

10. Each canoe in the picture has a hole in the front. One canoe will sink very fast. One canoe will sink slowly. One canoe will not sink.

   a. Which canoe will sink fast? _B_

   b. Which canoe will not sink? _C_

   c. Which canoe will sink slowly? _A_

   d. Which picture shows Jane paddling across the lake? _____

A   B   C

Skill items

11. Here's a rule: **If it is round, it will roll.**

   a. A gleem is round. So what else do you know about a gleem?
it will roll

   b. A rab is round. So what else do you know about a rab?
it will roll

LESSON 10

A

Story items

1. **Finish the sentence.** Felt is a kind of _cloth_.

2. Most felt-tipped pens do not have an eraser. Tell why.
   Ink is hard to erase

3. Look at the picture of the felt-tipped pen.

   a. Write these names on the picture:

   shaft   felt tip   ink

   b. The pen in the picture does not have an eraser. **Make an X** to show where an eraser would go on the pen.

   a. _That's the felt tip_
   b.
   c. _shaft_

Review items

4. **Draw a box around** the picture that shows a forest.

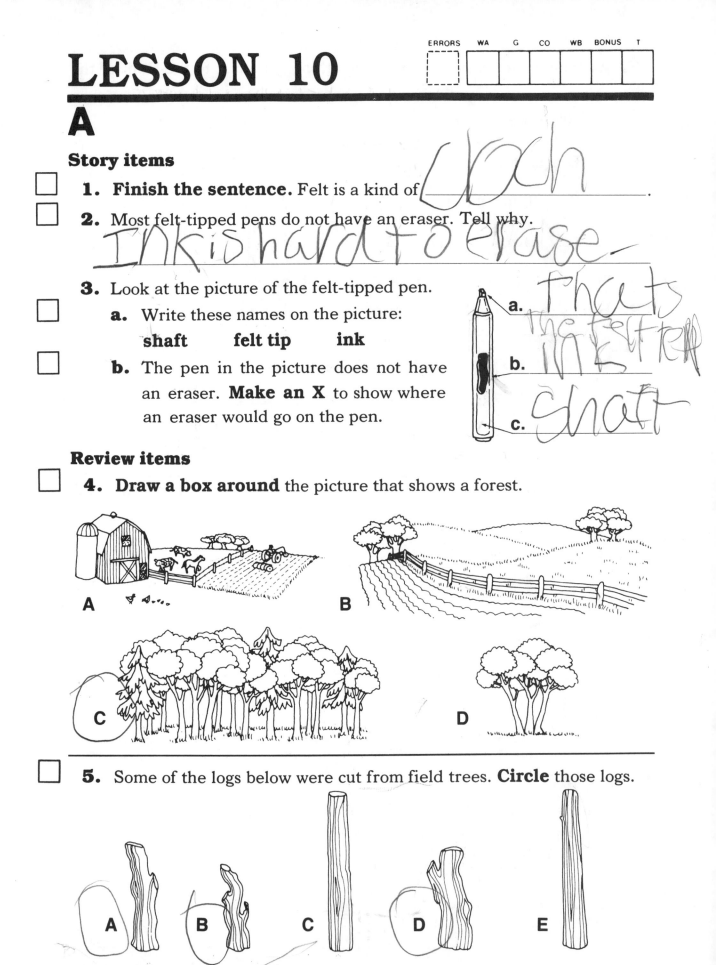

   A   B   C   D

5. Some of the logs below were cut from field trees. **Circle** those logs.

   A   B   C   D   E

6. Look at the picture below.

    a. Make an arrow **over each canoe** to show which way the canoe is moving.

    b. Make an arrow **under each paddle** to show which way the paddle is moving in the water.

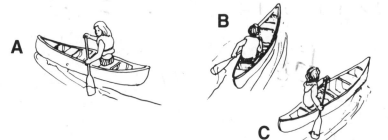

7. Look at the picture.

    a. **Make a T** at the **top** of the paddle to show where one hand would grab the paddle.

    b. **Make an M** in the **middle** of the paddle to show where the other hand would grab the paddle.

8. a. **Finish the rule** about the waves a canoe makes. The faster a canoe moves, _The waves it makes_ .

    b. Look at the picture below. One canoe is moving very fast. Write the letter of that canoe. _____

    c. One canoe is not moving at all. Write the letter of that canoe. _____

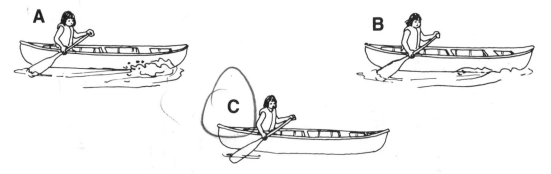

9. Name two kinds of canoes that Indians made.

① _dugout_ ② _bark_

10. Look at the picture below.

    a. Which letter is on the path? _D_

    b. Which letter is in the middle of the lake? _E_

    c. Which letter is on the shore

       of the lake? _N_

    d. Which letter is in the field?

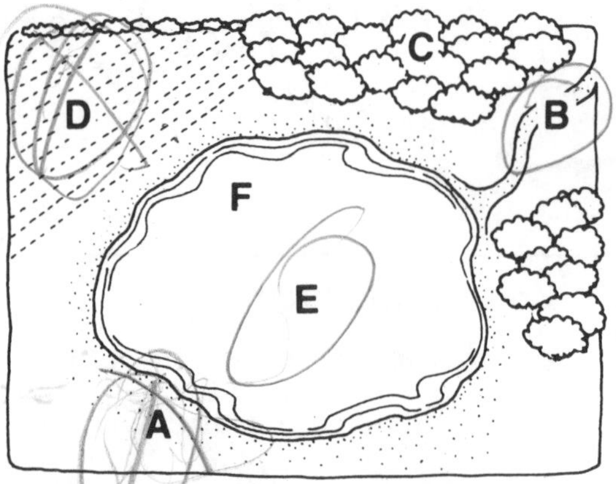

       _D_

11. a. What's the name of pretty flowers that grow in the water?

    water lilis

    b. Name two colors that those pretty flowers can be.

    ① _Pink and_ ② _yellow_

12. Each canoe in the picture below has a hole in the front. One canoe will sink very fast. One canoe will sink slowly. One canoe will not sink.

    a. Which canoe will sink fast? _A_

    b. Which canoe will not sink? _B_

    c. Which canoe will sink slowly? _C_

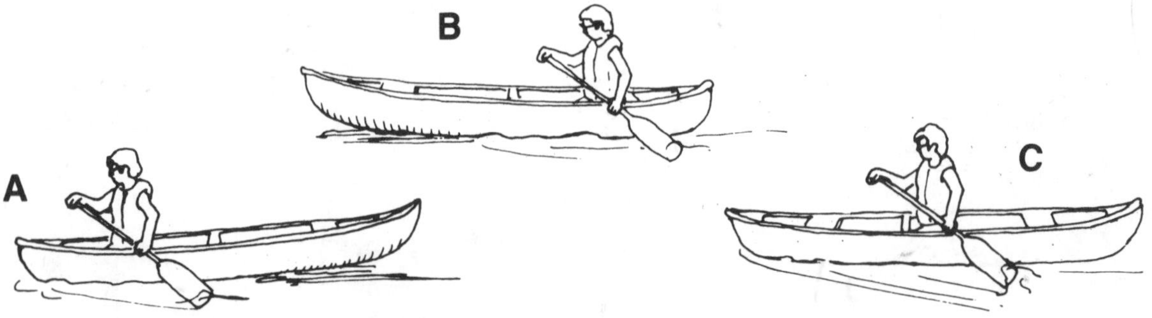

LESSON 11

A

Story items

1. **a.** What color was Joe Williams? _red_

   b. What kind of tip did Joe Williams have? _Fat_

2. What kind of job did Joe have? _construction_

3. Name three other members of the construction team.
   ① _Paint_ ② _brosh_ ③ _eraser_
   desk

4. Where did Joe live? _desk_

5. Did Mary think that Joe could get a new job? _no_

6. **a.** One of the things in the picture could be Joe's wife. **Circle** the object that could be Joe's wife.

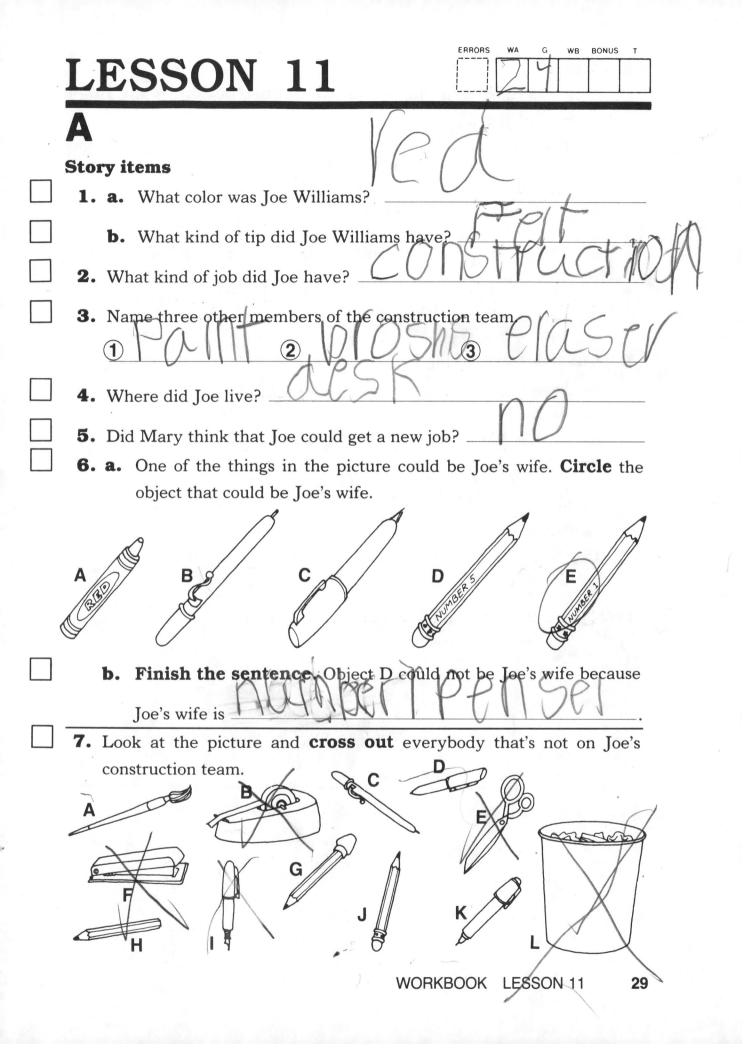

   A RED B C D NUMBER 5 E NUMBER 1

   b. **Finish the sentence.** Object D could not be Joe's wife because Joe's wife is _number 1 penser_.

7. Look at the picture and **cross out** everybody that's not on Joe's construction team.

   A B C D E F G H I J K L

Skill items

8. Here's a rule: **Everybody on the construction team helps make pictures.**

□　　**a.** The paint is on the construction team. So what else do you know about the paint? _help make pictures_

□　　**b.** The pencil is on the construction team. So what else do you know about the pencil? _help make pictures_

9. Underline everything Joe said in each item.

□　　**a.** Joe said, "I'm tired of making red lines."
□　　**b.** Joe said, "Our team works hard."
□　　**c.** "I must do something else," Joe said.
□　　**d.** "What job can I get?" Joe asked.
□　　**e.** Joe asked, "Can I find a new job?"

Review items

□　**10.** **Circle** the pictures of animals that are make-believe.

A B C D E F

□　**11.** Some of the trees below grew in a forest. **Circle** those trees.

A B 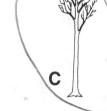 C D

30　　LESSON 11　WORKBOOK

12. Look at the picture of the felt-tipped pen.

a. Write these names on the picture:

   shaft   felt tip   ink

b. The pen in the picture does not have an eraser. **Make an X** to show where an eraser would go if the pen had an eraser.

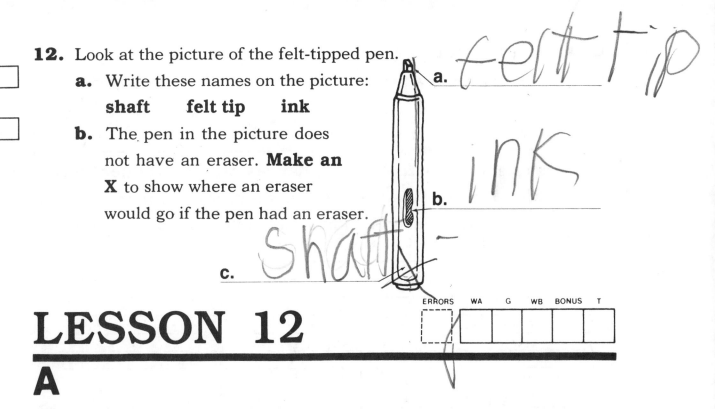

a. _felt tip_

c. _shaft_

b. _ink_

ERRORS	WA	G	WB	BONUS	T

LESSON 12

A

In today's lesson, you read about centimeters. Use what you learned to do this item.

1. Some lines in the box below are **not** one centimeter long.

   Cross out every line that is **not** one centimeter long.

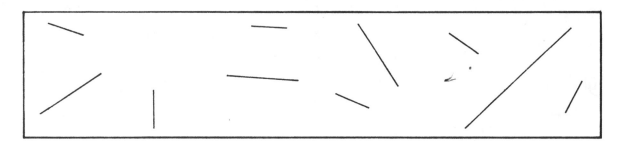

B

Story items

2. What color was Joe Williams? _red_

3. How did Joe get marks on him? _Mary drew_

4. Did Joe get a new job? _ing_

5. What was Joe's new job? _Warking as a_

6. a. How far apart were Joe's marks? _cetmete_

□
□ **b. Circle** the arrow that shows how far apart Joe's marks were.

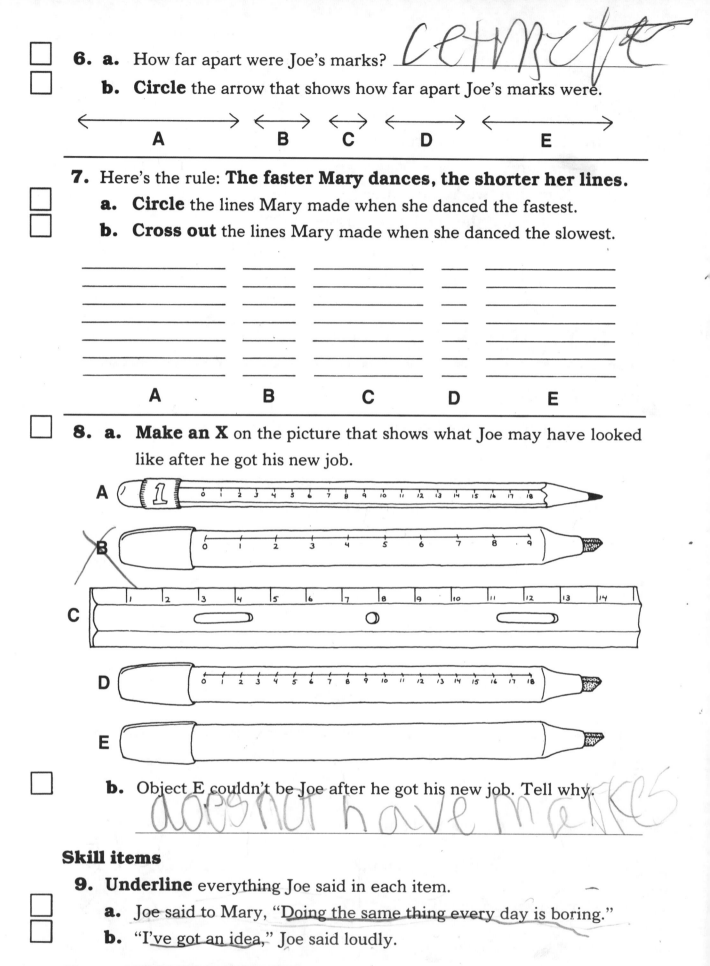

⟷	⟷	⟷	⟷	⟷
A	**B**	**C**	**D**	**E**

7. Here's the rule: **The faster Mary dances, the shorter her lines.**

□ **a. Circle** the lines Mary made when she danced the fastest.
□ **b. Cross out** the lines Mary made when she danced the slowest.

A   B   C   D   E

□ **8. a. Make an X** on the picture that shows what Joe may have looked like after he got his new job.

A

B

C

D

E

□ **b.** Object E couldn't be Joe after he got his new job. Tell why. _does not have merkes_

Skill items

9. Underline everything Joe said in each item.

□ **a.** Joe said to Mary, "Doing the same thing every day is boring."
□ **b.** "I've got an idea," Joe said loudly.

c. Joe said, "Make marks on me. Make marks all down my side."

d. "Make marks," Joe told Mary, "that are one centimeter apart."

e. "I'm here," Joe replied, "because I'm a ruler now."

10. Here's a rule: **All the flat rulers work on Saturday.**

a. Pete is a flat ruler. So what else do you know about Pete? _____

He weriks on satrday

b. Jane is a flat ruler. So what else do you know about Jane? _____

H werks on satrday

Review items

11. Look at the picture of the felt-tipped pen.

a. Write these names on the picture:

ink   **felt tip**   **shaft**

a. _____ *felt tip*

b. _____ *ink tip*

c. _____ *shaft*

b. The pen in the picture does not have an eraser. **Make an X** to show where an eraser would go if the pen had an eraser.

12. Some of the trees below grew in a forest. **Underline** those trees.

A   B   C   D   E

LESSON 13

A

In today's lesson, you read about beagles. Use what you learned to do these items.

☐ **1. Circle** all the beagles in the picture.

A   B   C   D

E   F   G   H

spots

☐ **2.** Dog C is not a beagle. Tell why. _____

_____

B

Story items

☐ **3.** Name three things that Jokey ate that other dogs didn't eat.

① *whit*   ② *brown*   ③ *black*

☐ **4. Finish the sentence.** The cat told Jokey, "The more you eat,

The tatter youget ."

5. The people who owned Jokey got madder and madder as Jokey got fatter and fatter. **Circle** the Jokey that made the owners the maddest.

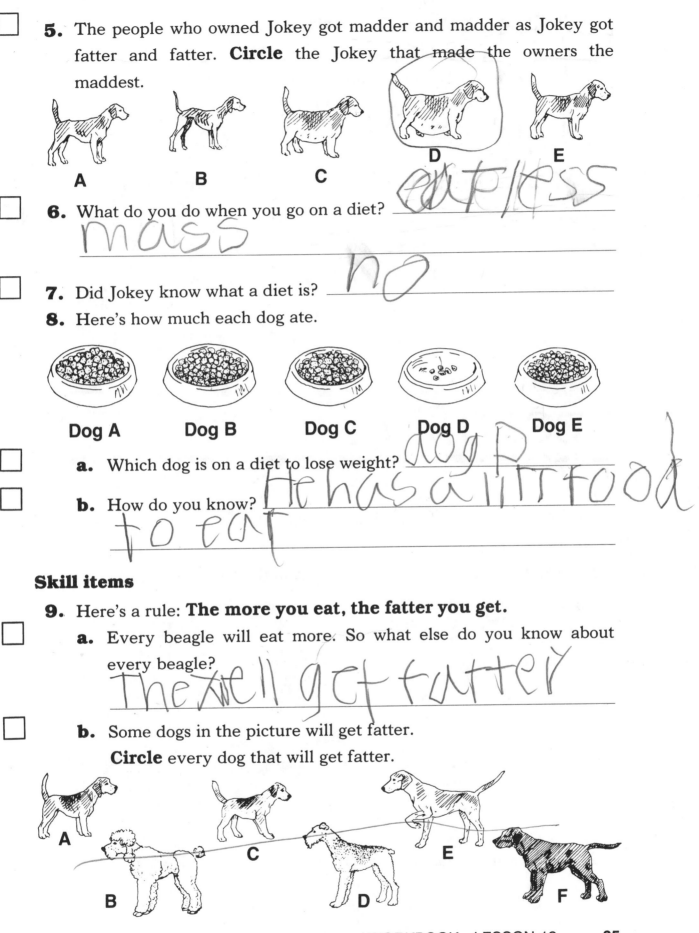

A   B   C   D   E

eat/ess

6. What do you do when you go on a diet? _____

mass

no

7. Did Jokey know what a diet is? _____

8. Here's how much each dog ate.

Dog A   Dog B   Dog C   Dog D   Dog E

a. Which dog is on a diet to lose weight? *dog D*

b. How do you know? *He has a littl food to eat*

Skill items

9. Here's a rule: **The more you eat, the fatter you get.**

a. Every beagle will eat more. So what else do you know about every beagle? *The well get fatter*

b. Some dogs in the picture will get fatter.

Circle every dog that will get fatter.

A   B   C   D   E   F

10. Underline everything Jokey said in each item.

a. "If I stop eating," Jokey said sadly, "I'll be hungry."

b. Jokey said, "I can't help it. It's not my fault."

c. "What's a diet?" Jokey asked.

d. Jokey told the cat, "I like to eat lots of things. I like dog food and mops."

e. "I'm so heavy," Jokey said slowly, "I can hardly move."

Review items

11. Some lines in the box below are one centimeter long. **Circle** every line that is one centimeter long.

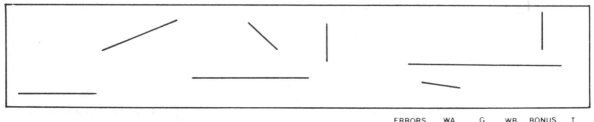

LESSON 14

ERRORS	WA	G	WB	BONUS	T
	2				

A

In today's lesson, you read about poodles. Use what you learned to do these items.

1. Underline all the standard poodles in the picture.

A   B   C   D

E   F   G   H

2. Dog F is not a standard poodle. Tell why. _It dosen't_ _have polar ears._

x

x

B

Story items

☐ **3. Finish the sentence.**

In the last story, the cat told Jokey, "The more you eat, _The_ _eater you get_"

Jokey eat to muc

☐ **4.** Why was Jokey so fat? _eat less_

☐ **5.** What do you do when you go on a diet? _Food_

☐ **6.** Where did Jokey go to lose weight? _heth spa_

☐ **7.** What kind of dogs ran the health spa? _stanerd poodl_

ard

☐ **8.** The picture below shows some of the dogs that ran the spa. **Circle** the dogs that ran the spa.

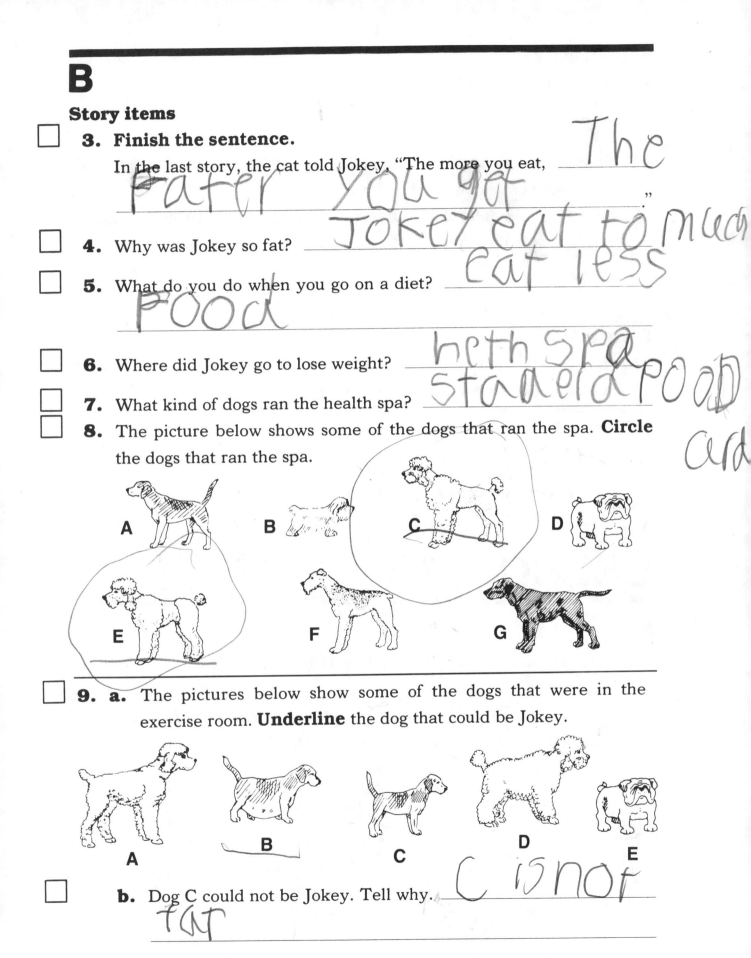

☐ **9. a.** The pictures below show some of the dogs that were in the exercise room. **Underline** the dog that could be Jokey.

☐ **b.** Dog C could not be Jokey. Tell why. _C isnot_

fat

Skill items

☐ **10. Circle everything the rat said.**

"That beagle is so fat," the rat said, "he can't jump one centimeter off the ground."

☐ **11. Underline everything the cat said.** "Come on," the cat said, "let's see you leap up and grab this tail."

☐ **12.** Here's a rule: **The dogs that ran the spa were in good shape.** Dolly was a dog that ran the spa. So what else do you know about Dolly?

in a good shape

Review items

☐ **13.** Some lines in the box below are **not** one centimeter long. **Cross out** the lines that are **not** one centimeter long.

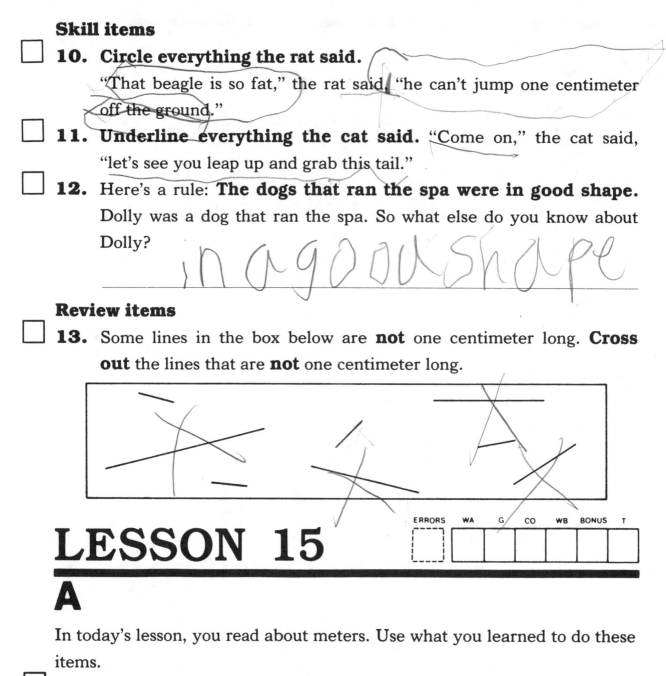

LESSON 15

ERRORS	WA	G	CO	WB	BONUS	T

A

In today's lesson, you read about meters. Use what you learned to do these items.

☐ **1.** Some people in the picture are holding sticks that are one meter long. Write **1 meter** next to each stick that is one meter long.

2. Look at the picture. The man is holding a stick that is one meter long.

☐ **a.** Write the letter of each object that is one meter long.

D B

☐ **b.** Write the letter of each object that is two meters long.

HA and6

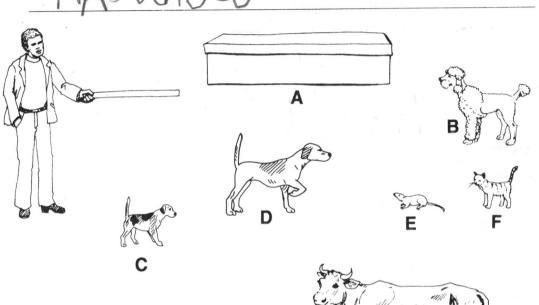

A

B

D

E F

C

G H

☐ **3.** If a poodle is one meter long, how many centimeters long is the

poodle? *100 setneters*

B

Story items

☐ **4.** Where did Jokey go to lose weight? *Hleth spa*

☐ **5.** What kind of dogs ran that place? *poodles*

☐ **6.** What was the good news that a white poodle gave Jokey? *slem and tream inno fin*

at all

7. Part of the poodle's bad news told how much Jokey could eat.

How much? _nutren_

8. What was the first thing Jokey had to do for an hour every day?

run

9. What was the other thing Jokey had to do for an hour every day?

do exrsisc

10. Name three exercises that Jokey couldn't do.

① _Tuch his tial_

② _Push up_

③ _Accdent_

11. Why did Jokey want to quit his diet? _he was tird_

12. Why didn't Jokey quit his diet? _Cat a bul the diet with_

Skill items

13. The fat beagles have to exercise for an hour every day.

Circle the dogs that must exercise for an hour every day.

A   B   C

D   E   F

14. Underline everything the poodle said. The white poodle told Jokey, "You can be slim and trim in no time at all."

15. Here are titles for different stories.

- Slim Jim's Super Diet.
- How to Make Ice Cream
- Joe Buys a Horse

☐ **a.** One story tells about something that is sweet. What's the title of that story?

How to make ice cream

☐ **b.** One story tells about how to lose weight. What's the title of that story?

Swim Jim's super diet

☐ **c.** One story tells about someone who got a new pet. What's the title of that story?

Jou buya Huse

Review items

☐ **16. a.** **Cross out** all the beagles in the picture.

☐ **b.** Dog D is not a beagle. Tell why. _____

_____

A   B   C

D   E   F   G

LESSON 16

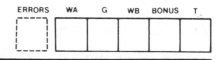
A

In today's lesson, you read about diets.

Use what you learned to do these items.

1. Everybody in the picture below should be on a diet. Under each person, write what kind of diet the person should be on.

   • Write **L** for a diet **to lose weight.**

   • Write **P** for a diet **to put on weight.**

   • Write **H** for a diet **to stay healthy.**

A   B   C   D   E

B

Story items

2. While Jokey was on his diet, what was he supposed to eat? _nothing_

3. Name two things Jokey had to do for an hour every day.

   ① _run_   ② _exrsie_

4. How many days did Jokey stay on his diet? _4_

5. Name three things that Jokey ate when he went off his diet.

   ① _busket_ ② _boxes_ ③ _bags_

6. Who did Jokey see on his way home? _the black cat_

7. **a.** Did Jokey chase the cat? _no_

   b. Why not? _Jocy is too fat_

8. a. Finish the sentence. As Jokey walked home, he said to himself,

"I'll never go _OFF my diet_

no di esen"

b. Why did he say that? _no di esen_

9. Circle the picture that could be Jokey **before** he went off his diet.

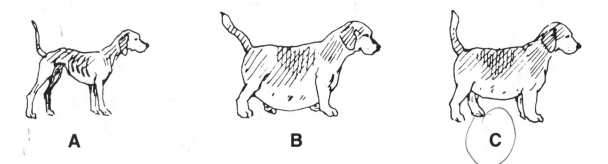

A   B   C

Skill items

10. Here's a rule: **Every black cat teases Jokey.**

a. Slick is a black cat. So what else do you know about Slick? _____

teases Jokey

b. Sam is a black cat. So what else do you know about Sam? _____

teases Jokey

11. Make a line over everything the cat said.

"Here it is," the cat said, and she held her tail high in the air. "Just run right over here and take a big bite."

Review items

12. Some people in the picture are holding sticks that are one meter long. Write **1 meter** under each stick that is one meter long.

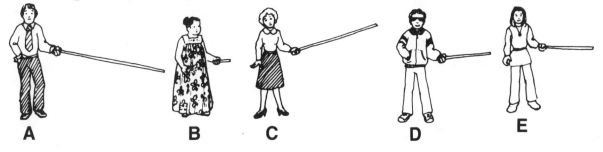

A   B   C   D   E

13. How many centimeters are in one meter? _____

14. a. Cross out all the standard poodles in the picture.

    b. Dog D is not a standard poodle. Tell why. _____

A   B   C   D

E   F   G   H

LESSON 17

ERRORS	WA	G	WB	BONUS	T

A In today's lesson, you read about pointers. Use what you learned to do these items.

1. Look at the picture.

A   B   C   D

E   F   G   H

    a. Circle every dog that is a pointer.

    b. Write the word **point** over every pointer that is pointing.

    c. Dog C is not a pointer. Tell two reasons why.

        ① _____

        ② _____

2. How many centimeters long is a pointer? _____

B

Story items

3. When a beagle is very skinny, which bones can you see? _____

_____

4. How did Jokey feel about himself after he lost some weight?

_____

5. After Jokey lost some weight, he could do some things that he hadn't been able to do for a long time.

Name three of those things.

① _____

② _____

③ _____

6. How high could the pointer jump? **Underline the answer.**
- 10 centimeters   • 1 meter   • 2 meters

7. How high could the white poodle jump? **Circle the answer.**
- 10 centimeters   • 1 meter   • 2 meters

8. Did the cat ever tease Jokey again? _____

9. **Circle** the picture that shows what Jokey looked like after dieting for two months.

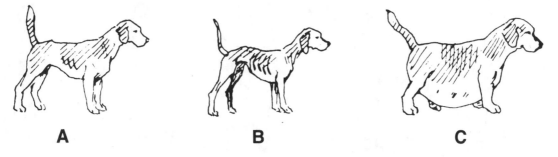

A   B   C

Skill items

10. Here's a rule: **Every pointer could jump two meters off the ground.**

    a. Zack is a pointer. So what else do you know about Zack? _____

    _____

    b. Bert is a pointer. So what else do you know about Bert? _____

    _____

11. Underline everything Jokey said.

    "Watch out," Jokey said to the cat, "or I'll jump up on that fence and take a bite out of your tail."

Review items

12. Look at the lines in the box below.

    a. Write **1** on each line that is one centimeter long.

    b. Write **3** on each line that is three centimeters long.

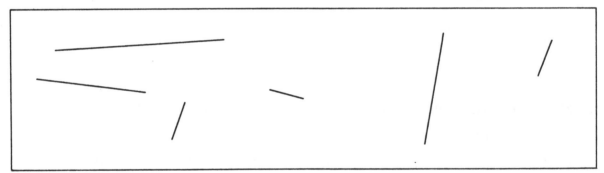

13. Everybody in the picture below should be on a diet.

    Write what kind of diet each person should be on.

    • Write **L** for a diet **to lose weight.**

    • Write **P** for a diet **to put on weight.**

    • Write **H** for a diet **to stay healthy.**

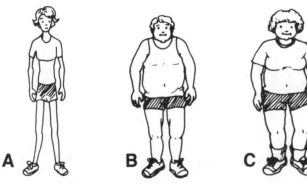

A   B   C   D   E

14. Look at the picture. The man is holding a stick that is one meter long.

a. Write the letter of each object that is one meter long.

_____

b. Write the letter of each object that is two meters long.

_____

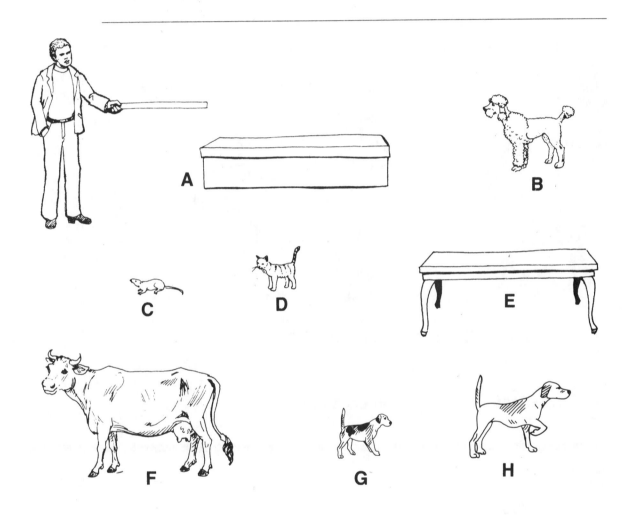

LESSON 18

A

In today's lesson, you read about reindeer.

Use what you learned to do these items.

1. The man is holding a stick that is one meter long. All the animals that are one meter tall at the shoulder are reindeer.

   a. **Circle** all the reindeer in the picture.

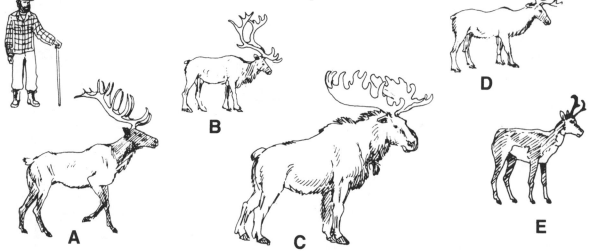

   b. Animal C is not a reindeer. Tell why. _____

_____

   c. **Circle** the antlers on each animal.

B

Story items

   2. Why did Santa get stuck? _____

   3. Who made big toys? **Underline the answer.**

   • Max   • Bix

   4. Who made little toys? **Circle the answer.**

   • Max   • Bix

5. Name the elves who came up with the plan that worked.

_____

6. Look at the picture and finish the sentence that the girl is saying.

I wonder why Santa
left this pair of

_____ _____

_____.

7. Circle the picture that could be Santa after he got out of the chimney.

A   B   C   D

Skill items

8. Here's a rule: **All elves make toys.**

   a. Rex is an elf. So what else do you know about Rex? _____

_____

   b. Pax is an elf. So what else do you know about Pax? _____

_____

9. Circle everything Max said.

Max told Santa, "Pull with your hands and push with your feet."

Review items

10. Some lines in the box below are one centimeter long.

Write **1 centimeter** next to each of those lines.

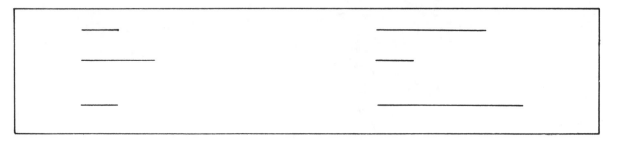

11. a. **Underline** every dog that is a pointer.

    b. Dog B is not a pointer. Tell why. _____

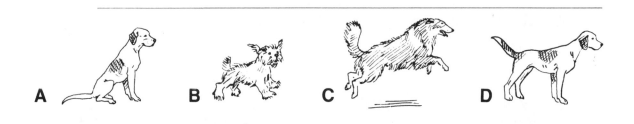

A   B   C   D

12. Look at the picture below.

    a. Make an arrow **over** each canoe to show which way the canoe is moving.

    b. Make an arrow **under** each paddle to show which way the paddle is moving in the water.

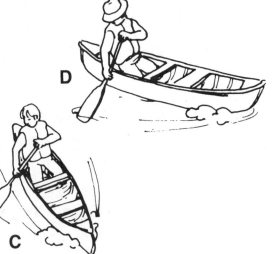

LESSON 19

A

In today's lesson, you read about fleas. Use what you learned to do these items.

1. A spider is not an insect because it doesn't have the right number of legs. Look at the picture of a spider. How many legs does a spider have? _____

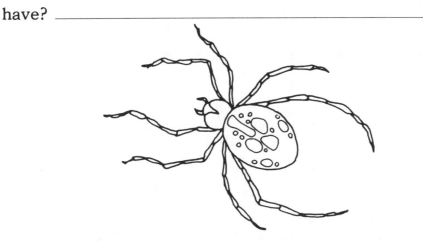

2. How many legs does an insect have? _____

3. How many legs does a flea have? _____

4. If a fly is an insect, what else do you know about a fly? _____

_____

B

Story items

5. In what year was Aunt Fanny's Flea Circus formed?
Circle the answer.   • 1963   • 1971   • 1990

6. In what year did Aunt Fanny and the fleas start to fight?
Underline the answer.   • 1963   • 1971   • 1990

7. Name three fleas that were in the circus. ①_____

②_____   ③_____

8. Draw a line from each flea's name to the objects the flea used in its act.

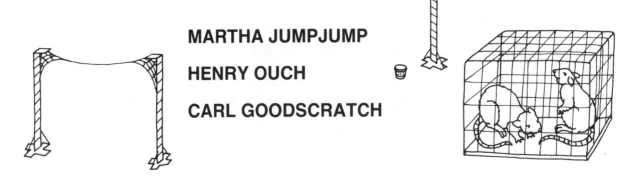

MARTHA JUMPJUMP

HENRY OUCH

CARL GOODSCRATCH

9. Name two reasons that the fleas were mad at Aunt Fanny.

① _____

② _____

10. Where did the fleas live? _____

11. Where did Aunt Fanny live? _____

12. **Circle** the picture of the object where the fleas lived.

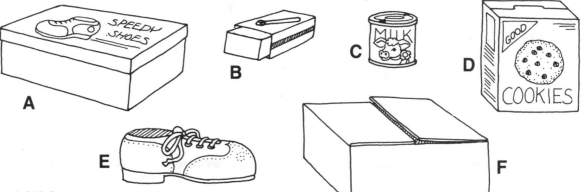

Skill items

13. Underline everything the fleas said.

"No," all the other fleas agreed. "Things must change."

14. Here's a rule: **Every person loved the flea circus.**

   a. Tom is a person. So what else do you know about Tom? _____

   _____

   b. Jean is a person. So what else do you know about Jean?

   _____

Review items

15. The man is holding a stick that is one meter long. All the animals that are 1 meter tall at the shoulder are reindeer.

    a. **Underline** all the reindeer in the picture.

    b. Animal B is not a reindeer. Tell why. _____

_____

    c. **Cross out** the antlers on each animal.

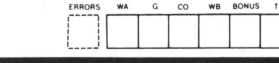

LESSON 20

ERRORS	WA	G	CO	WB	BONUS	T

A

In today's lesson, you read about four directions. Use what you learned to do these items.

1. Look at the map below. Follow the instructions.

  a. Write **north, south, east,** and **west** in the right boxes.

  b. Touch the X. An arrow goes from the X.

  Which direction is that arrow going? _____

  c. Touch the Y. An arrow goes from the Y.

  Which direction is that arrow going? _____

  d. Touch the B. An arrow goes from the B.

  Which direction is that arrow going? _____

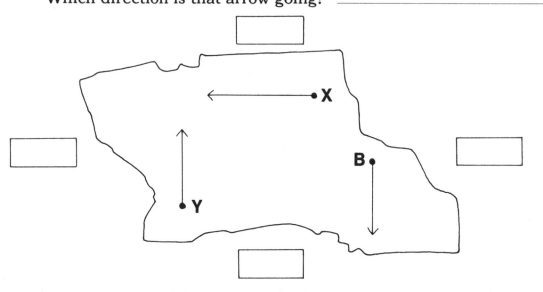

B

Story items

  2. Name two reasons that the fleas were mad at Aunt Fanny.

  ① _____

  ② _____

  3. a. Were the fleas in Aunt Fanny's flea circus **real fleas** or

  make-believe fleas? _____

  b. How do you know? _____

  _____

  4. Where do the fleas in flea circuses usually come from?

  _____

5. What's the first thing that fleas must be taught?

_____

6. Name two other things that fleas have been taught to do.

① _____

② _____

Skill items

7. Here are titles for different stories.

- 100 Ways to Cook Turkey   • A Funny Story
- Why Smoking Will Hurt You

a. One story tells about reading something that makes you laugh. What's the title of that story?

_____

b. One story tells about something that is bad for you. What's the

title of that story? _____

c. One story tells about how to make different meals out of one thing. What's the title of that story?

_____

Review items

8. Some of the logs below were cut from field trees. **Cross out** those logs.

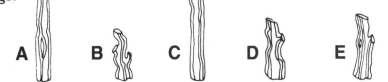

A   B   C   D   E   F

9. Look at the picture of a paddle.

a. Make a **T** at the top of the paddle to show where one hand would grab the paddle.

b. Make an **M** in the middle of the paddle to show where the other hand would grab the paddle.

10. Some lines in the box below are one centimeter long. Write **1 centimeter** next to each of those lines.

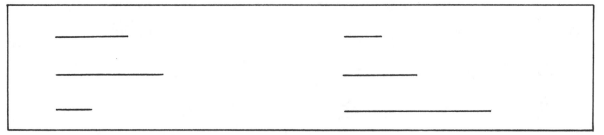

11. a. Make a box around each beagle in the picture.

    b. Dog A is not a beagle. Tell why. _____

_____

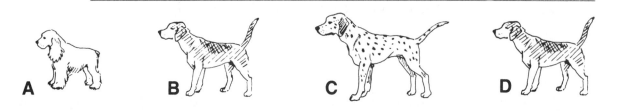

12. Look at the picture. The man is holding a stick that is one meter long.

    a. Write the letter of each object that is one meter long. _____

    b. Write the letter of each object that is two meters long. _____

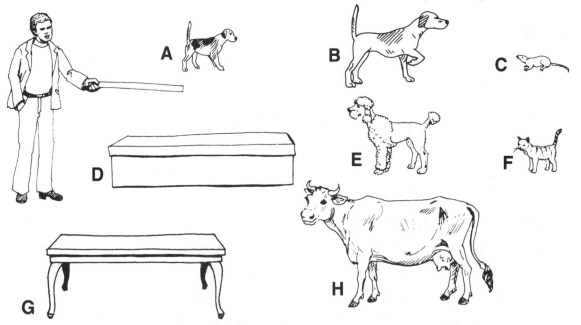

13. How many centimeters are in one meter? _____

14. a. Underline every dog that is a pointer.

    b. Dog C is not a pointer. Tell why. _____

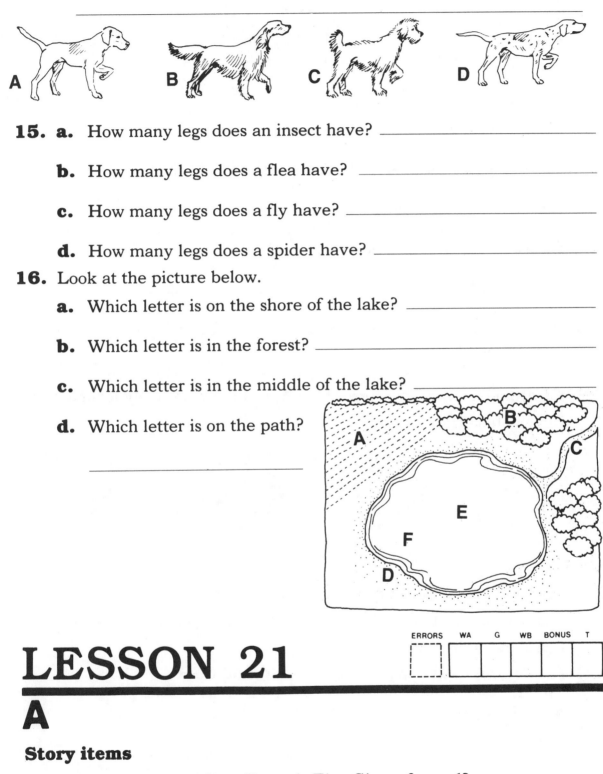

15. a. How many legs does an insect have? _____

    b. How many legs does a flea have? _____

    c. How many legs does a fly have? _____

    d. How many legs does a spider have? _____

16. Look at the picture below.

    a. Which letter is on the shore of the lake? _____

    b. Which letter is in the forest? _____

    c. Which letter is in the middle of the lake? _____

    d. Which letter is on the path?

LESSON 21

ERRORS	WA	G	WB	BONUS	T

A

Story items

    1. In what year was Aunt Fanny's Flea Circus formed? _____

    2. In what year did Aunt Fanny and the fleas start to fight? _____

3. The picture shows what each flea did. Write the name for each flea.

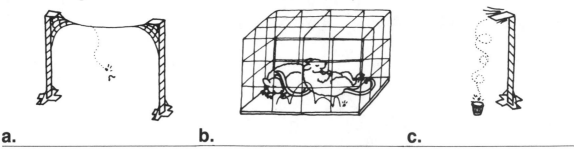

a. _____ b. _____ c. _____

4. a. Did Aunt Fanny change her ways? _____

b. Which flea made Aunt Fanny say she would change? _____

5. Why is Aunt Fanny happy now? _____

6. Where do the fleas live now? _____

7. Where did they used to live? _____

8. Why are the fleas happy now? _____

_____

9. Circle the picture that shows how Aunt Fanny probably looked after Martha fell off the wire.

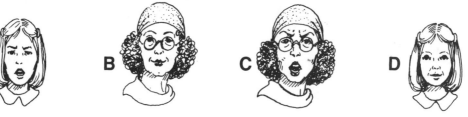

A   B   C   D

Skill items

10. Make a line over everything Aunt Fanny said.

"Ladies and gentlemen," Aunt Fanny said, "welcome to the greatest flea show in the world."

11. Here's a rule: **All the people got mad and booed.**

a. Tim is a person. So what else do you know about Tim?

_____

b. Liz is a person. So what else do you know about Liz?

_____

Review items

12. **a.** Where do the fleas in flea circuses usually come from?

_____

b. What's the first thing that fleas must be taught?

_____

c. Name two other things that fleas have been taught to do.

① _____ ② _____

13. Look at the map below. Follow these instructions.

a. Write **north, south, east,** and **west** in the right boxes.

b. Touch the R. An arrow goes from the R. Which direction is that

arrow going? _____

c. Make an arrow that goes east from the X.

d. Make an arrow that goes west from the T.

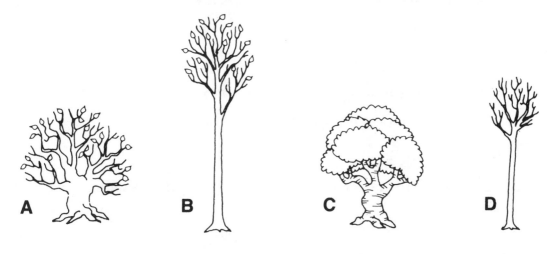

14. Some of the trees below grew in a forest. **Circle** those trees.

A   B   C   D

LESSON 22

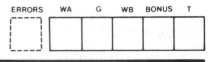

A

In today's lesson, you read about telling how two objects are the same. Use what you learned to do this item.

1. Look at object A and object B. Write three ways both objects are the same.

① _____

② _____

③ _____

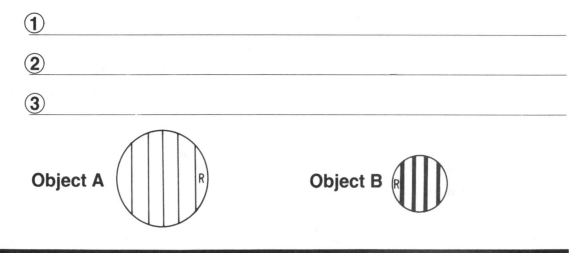

Object A   Object B

B

Skill items

2. Here's a rule: **Big men are heavy.**

   a. Big men are heavy. An elephant is **not** a big man.
     So what else do you know about an elephant?

     _____

   b. Big men are heavy. A whale is **not** a big man.
     So what else do you know about a whale?

     _____

   c. Big men are heavy. Jack is a big man.
     So what else do you know about Jack?

     _____

   d. Big men are heavy. Bob is **not** a big man. So what else do you

     know about Bob? _____

3. Here's a new rule: **Dogs have hair.**

    a. Dogs have hair. A girl is not a dog. So what else do you know

    about a girl? _____

    b. Dogs have hair. Jokey is a dog. So what else do you know about
    Jokey?

    _____

    c. Dogs have hair. A cat is not a dog. So what else do you know

    about a cat? _____

Review items

4. Look at the picture below.

    a. Make an arrow **over** each canoe to show which way the canoe is
    moving.

    b. Make an arrow **under** each paddle to show which way the paddle
    is moving in the water.

5. Look at the lines in the box below.

    a. Write a **2** next to each line that is two centimeters long.

    b. Write a **3** next to each line that is three centimeters long.

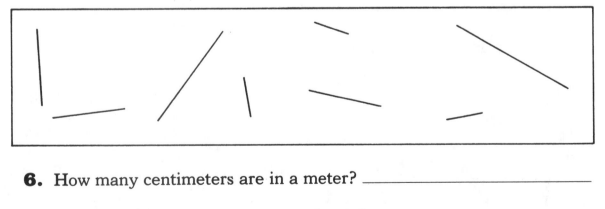

6. How many centimeters are in a meter? _____

7. a. How many legs does an insect have? _____

    b. How many legs does a flea have? _____

8. **Cross out** the picture that shows a forest.

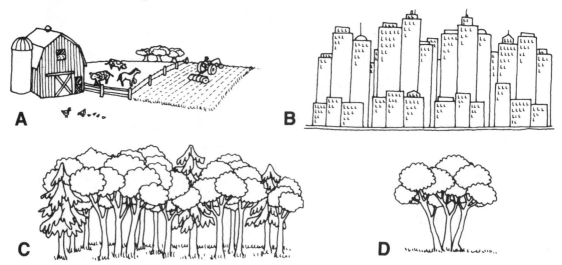

A B C D

9. **a.** **Circle** all the standard poodles in the picture.

b. Dog C is not a standard poodle. Tell why. _____

A B C D

10. The man is holding a stick that is one meter long. All the animals that are 1 meter tall at the shoulder are reindeer.

a. **Underline** all the reindeer in the picture.

b. Animal A is not a reindeer. Tell why. _____

c. **Circle** the antlers on each animal.

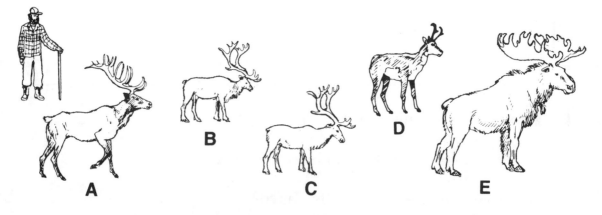

A B C D E

11. Look at the picture of a paddle.

    a. Make a **T** at the top of the paddle to show where one hand would grab the paddle.

    b. Make an **M** in the middle of the paddle to show where the other hand would grab the paddle.

---

12. Some of the trees below grew in a forest.
Make a box around those trees.

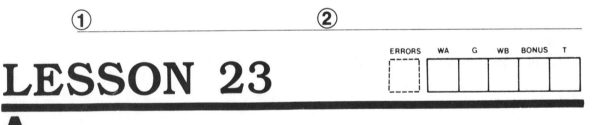

13. a. What's the name of pretty flowers that grow in the water?

    _____

    b. Name two colors that those pretty flowers can be.

    ① _____   ② _____

LESSON 23

ERRORS	WA	G	WB	BONUS	T

A

In today's lesson, you read about toads and frogs.

Use what you learned to do these items.

  1. Circle the animals that live on the land.

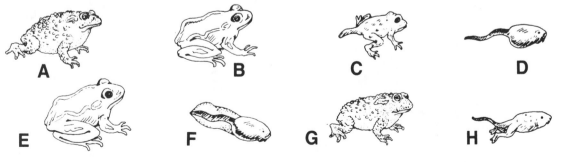

2. Some things happen as tadpoles grow.

    a. Circle what happens first.

    b. Underline what happens last.

  • Their tail disappears. • They grow front legs. • They grow back legs.

B

Story items

3. What kind of animal was Goad? _____

4. a. Name the lake that Goad lived near.

    _____

    b. Why was it called that?

    _____

5. Finish the sentence.

    When Goad was in the water, she was not _____.

6. What did Goad hop over near the south shore of the lake?

    _____

7. What did Goad like to do near the east shore of the lake?

    _____

8. Name two reasons people wanted to catch Goad.

    ① _____

    ② _____

9. Circle the animal that could be Goad.

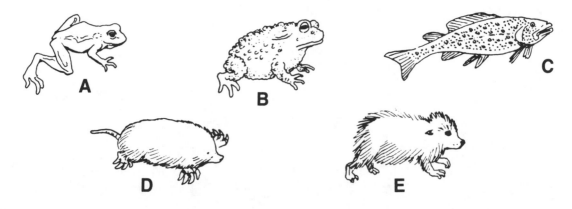

A   B   C   D   E

10. Hunters from a zoo made three of the statements below.

Underline those three statements.

- "I'd sure like to catch that toad."
- "Let's shoot it dead."
- "That toad would make a good dinner."
- "We must not hurt that toad."
- "Let's use a net to catch Goad."

Skill items

11. Look at object A, object B, and object C. Write two ways all three objects are the same.

① _____

② _____

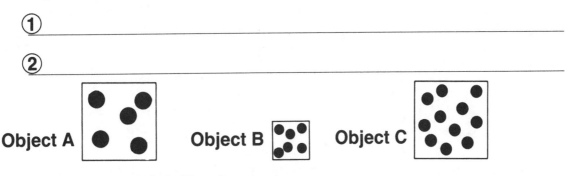

Object A   Object B   Object C

12. Here's a rule: **Fish live in water.**

   a. Fish live in water. A trout is a fish. So what else do you know

   about a trout? _____

   b. Fish live in water. A frog is not a fish. So what else do you know

   about a frog? _____

   c. Fish live in water. A whale is not a fish. So what else do you

   know about a whale? _____

   d. Fish live in water. A turtle is not a fish. So what else do you

   know about a turtle? _____

Review items

13. a. What's the name of the pretty flowers that grow in the water?

   _____

   b. Name two colors that those pretty flowers can be.

   ① _____   ② _____

LESSON 24

A

In today's lesson, you read about how toads are different from frogs. Use what you learned to do these items.

1. Which animal can jump farther, a toad or a frog? _____

2. Which animal has teeth, a toad or a frog? _____

3. Circle the toads in the picture.

B

Story items

4. Fill in the blanks.

  a. Goad was hard to catch because she was very _____.

  b. She was also very _____.

  c. She was also very _____.

5. What did the hunters from Alaska use when they tried to catch

Goad? _____

6. What trick did Goad use to fool the hunters from Alaska?

_____

7. What part of Goad is white? _____

66 LESSON 24 WORKBOOK

8. Circle the picture that could be Goad using her first trick.

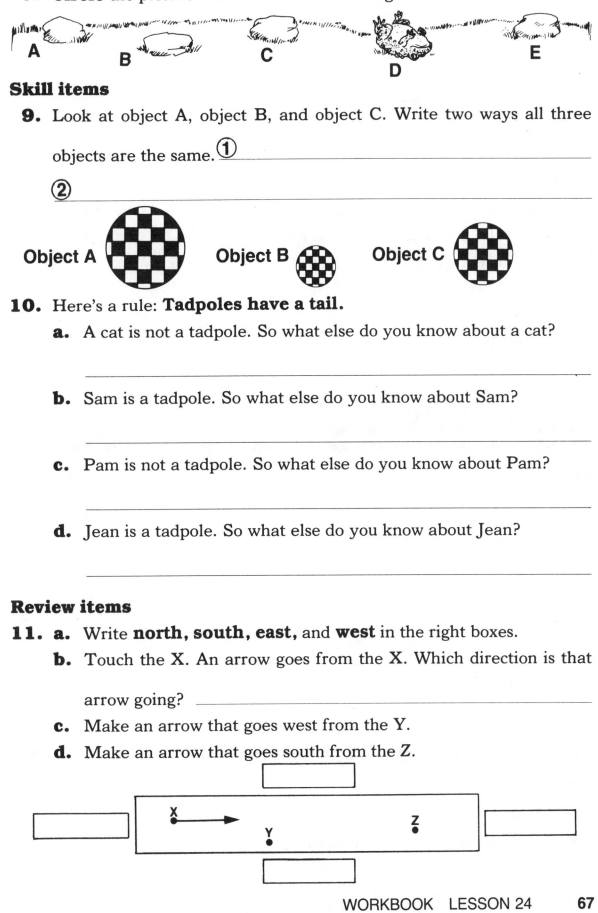

A   B   C   D   E

Skill items

9. Look at object A, object B, and object C. Write two ways all three

objects are the same. ① _____

② _____

Object A   **Object B**   **Object C**

10. Here's a rule: **Tadpoles have a tail.**

   a. A cat is not a tadpole. So what else do you know about a cat?

   _____

   b. Sam is a tadpole. So what else do you know about Sam?

   _____

   c. Pam is not a tadpole. So what else do you know about Pam?

   _____

   d. Jean is a tadpole. So what else do you know about Jean?

   _____

Review items

11. a. Write **north**, **south**, **east**, and **west** in the right boxes.

   b. Touch the X. An arrow goes from the X. Which direction is that

   arrow going? _____

   c. Make an arrow that goes west from the Y.

   d. Make an arrow that goes south from the Z.

12. Circle the animals that live on the land.

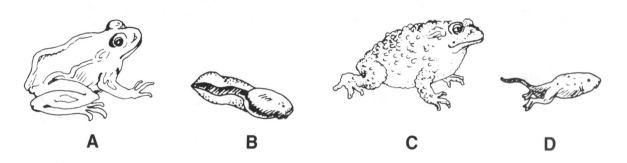

A   B   C   D

13. Some things happen as tadpoles grow.

  a. Make a box around what happens first.

  b. Underline what happens last.

   • Their tail disappears.

   • They grow back legs.

   • They grow front legs.

LESSON 25

ERRORS	WA	G	CO	WB	BONUS	T

A

In today's lesson, you learned how toads catch flies. Use what you learned to do these items.

  1. Name one insect toads eat. _____

  2. Finish the sentence. A toad catches flies with its _____.

  3. Why do flies stick to a toad's tongue?

  _____

  _____

B

Story items

  4. Write the word **make-believe** after each statement that could not be true.

a. A toad was as big as a pillow. _____

b. A toad could hop. _____

c. A toad ate flies. _____

d. A toad is smarter than a person. _____

5. Fill in the blank.

People in Toadsville said that Goad had escaped from over

_____ food traps.

6. Fill in the blank.

Goad had really escaped from _____
food traps.

7. Here's a picture of a food trap. The arrow shows the way the fly will move when the toad grabs it. Follow that arrow with your finger.

a. Draw an arrow to show which way the string moves at A.

b. Draw an arrow to show which way the stick moves at B.

Skill items

8. Here are titles for different stories.

- The Prancing Bear
- The Fly That Couldn't Fly
- How to Grow Water Lilies

a. One story tells about an insect that was different. What's the title of that story?

b. One story tells about an animal that walked on its tiptoes. What's the title of that story?

_____

c. One story tells about how to have pretty plants. What's the title of that story?

_____

Review items

9. Look at the picture below.

   a. Make an arrow **over** each canoe to show which way the canoe is moving.

   b. Make an arrow **under** each paddle to show which way the paddle is moving in the water.

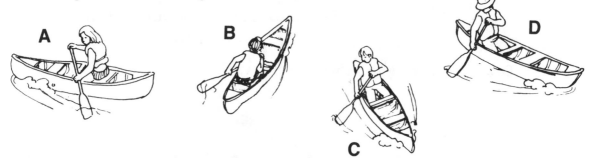

10. Some lines in the box below are one centimeter long.
Write **1 centimeter** next to each of those lines.

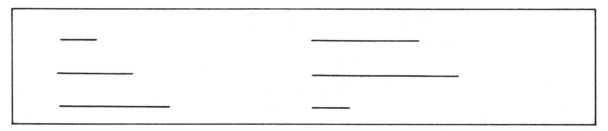

11. Some people in the picture are holding sticks that are one meter long. Write **1 meter** next to each stick that is one meter long.

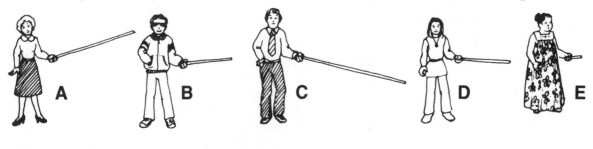

12. How many centimeters are in one meter? _____

13. a. How many legs does an insect have? _____

    b. How many legs does a flea have? _____

    c. How many legs does a fly have? _____

    d. How many legs does a spider have? _____

14. a. Where do the fleas in flea circuses usually come from?

_____

    b. What's the first thing that fleas must be taught?

_____

    c. Name two other things that fleas have been taught to do.

      ① _____ ② _____

15. Underline the toads in the picture.

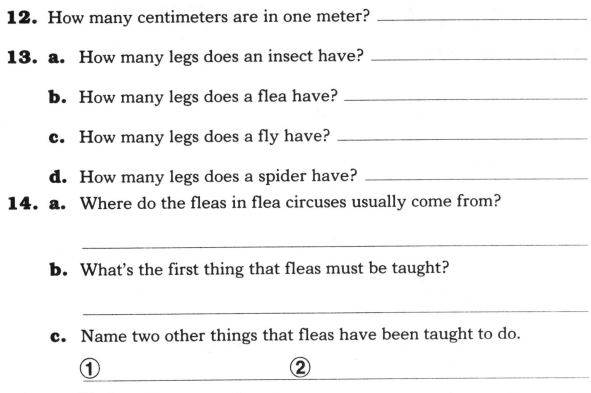

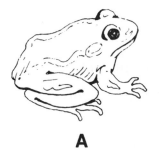

A

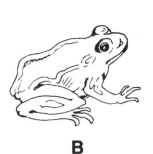

B

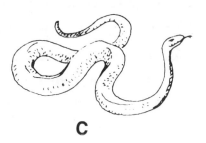

C

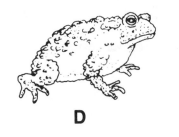

D

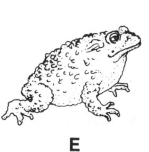

E

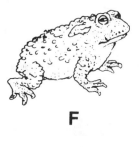

F

LESSON 26

A

In today's lesson, you read about moles.

Use what you learned to do this item.

1. Circle the moles in the picture below.

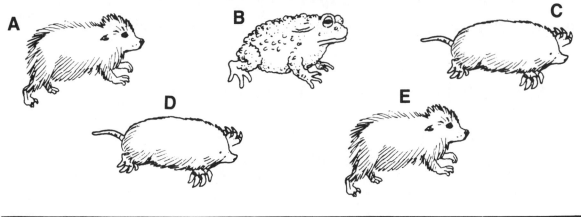

B

In today's lesson, you learned a rule about balloons.

Use what you learned to do this item.

2. a. Circle the balloon that lets the most light come through.

   b. Cross out the balloon that lets the least light come through.

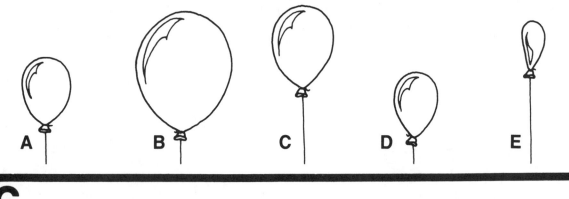

C

Story items

3. List Goad's four tricks for escaping from hunters.

First trick: _____

Second trick: _____

Third trick: _____

Fourth trick: _____

4. What do a mole's legs look like? _____

5. The man from England put his steel trap on a rock. Why did he put

it there? _____

6. What did the man from England put in his trap? _____

7. How did Goad get away from the famous steel trap? _____

_____

Skill items

8. Look at object A and object B. Write two ways that tell how both
objects are the same.

① _____

② _____

Object A   **Object B**

9. Here's a rule: **Toads are covered with warts.**

  a. Pete is not a toad. So what else do you know about Pete?

_____

  b. Goad is a toad. So what else do you know about Goad?

_____

  c. Fran is not a toad. So what else do you know about Fran?

_____

  d. Pat is not a toad. So what else do you know about Pat?

_____

Review items

10. Here's a picture of a food trap. The arrow shows the way the fly will move when the toad grabs it.

    a. **Draw an arrow** to show which way the string moves at A.

    b. **Draw an arrow** to show which way the stick moves at B.

11. a. Name one insect that toads eat. _____

    b. **Finish the sentence.**

      A toad catches insects with its _____.

12. Look at the picture.

    a. Make a **T** at the top of the paddle to show where one hand would grab the paddle.

    b. Make an **M** in the middle of the paddle to show where the other hand would grab the paddle.

LESSON 27

ERRORS	WA	G	WB	BONUS	T

A

In today's lesson, you read about binoculars.

Use what you learned to do these items.

    1. Here's what you see through the circles made by your hands.

    Draw what you would see through strong binoculars.

2. Here's what you see through strong binoculars.

Draw what you would see through the circles made by your hands.

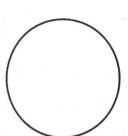

B

Story items

3. List Goad's four tricks for escaping from hunters.

First trick: _____

Second trick: _____

Third trick: _____

Fourth trick: _____

4. Name the trick that Goad used to get away from the hunters from

Alaska. _____

5. Name the trick that Goad used to get away from the famous steel

trap. _____

6. Draw an arrow at A and an arrow at B to show which way the string will move when the toad moves the blue fly.

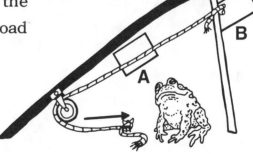

7. What is Goad's only weakness? _____

8. Why did people hope they would be around when Goad was

swimming in the lake? _____

9. Why did people use binoculars to look for Goad? _____

_____

10. How many people were in the Brown family? _____

Skill items

11. Look at object A and object B. Write two ways that tell how both objects are the same.

① _____

② _____

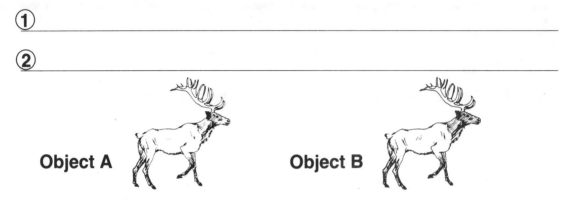

Object A   Object B

12. Here's a rule: **Trees have leaves.**

   a. A maple is a tree. So what else do you know about a maple?

   _____

   b. An oak is a tree. So what else do you know about an oak?

   _____

   c. A bush is not a tree. So what else do you know about a bush?

   _____

   d. A weed is not a tree. So what else do you know about a weed?

   _____

Review items

13. **Cross out** the moles in the picture.

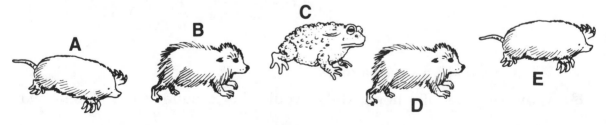

14. What do a mole's legs look like? _____

LESSON 28

A

In today's lesson, you read about how animals act when there is a fire. Use what you learned to do these items.

1. When wouldn't a fox bother a rabbit? _____

_____

2. What would the fox and rabbit do when there is a fire?

_____

B

In today's lesson, you read about smoke and wind. Use what you learned to do this item.

3. The arrow in each picture shows which way the wind is blowing.
   Draw the smoke in each picture.

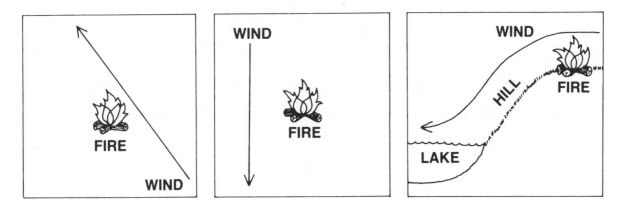

C

Story items

4. What is Goad's only weakness? _____

5. Why did people use binoculars to look for Goad? _____

_____

6. How many people were in the Brown family? _____

7. What did the mean grandmother do most of the time? _____

_____

8. Name three members of the Brown family. ①_____

②_____ ③_____

9. Did the people in Toadsville know what the Browns' plan was for

catching Goad? _____

10. a. Finish the sentence. The Browns' plan was to make Goad

think that _____.

b. What did the Browns burn to make the smoke? _____

Review items

11. How many centimeters are in a meter? _____

12. Here's what you see through the circles made by your hands.   Draw what you would see through strong binoculars.

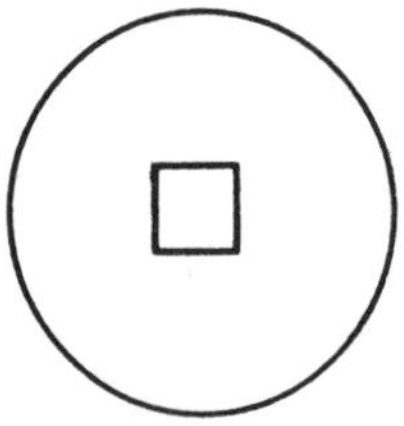

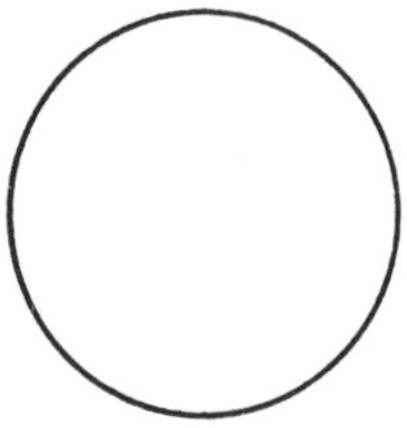

13. Look at the picture below.

a. Circle the balloon that lets the most light come through.

b. Underline the balloon that lets the least light come through.

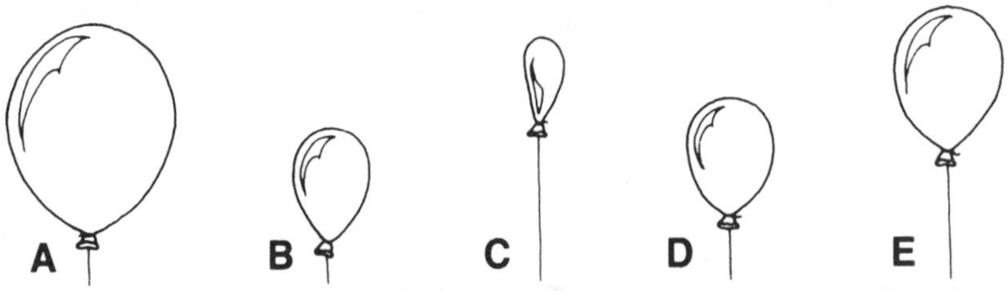

A   B   C   D   E

14. Draw an arrow at A and an arrow at B to show which way the
string will move when the toad
moves the blue fly.

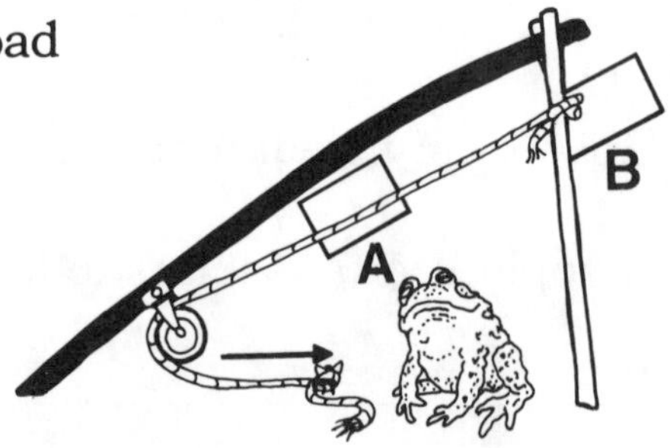

B

A

LESSON 29

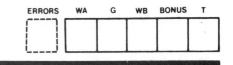

A

In today's lesson, you read about how air moves an object. Use what you learned to do these items.

1. a. Make a dotted arrow in the picture to show which way the air will leave the balloon.

   b. Make a solid arrow on the balloon to show which way it will move.

2. The dotted arrow shows the way the air leaves the jet engine. **Make a solid arrow** on the engine to show which way it will move.

B

Story items

3. What did Goad think was coming down the hill?

_____

4. What was really coming down the hill?

_____

5. What did Goad do when she smelled the smoke?

_____

6. How do people know how Goad got away from the Browns?

_____

7. What was Goad doing in the first snapshot? _____

8. What was Goad doing in the second snapshot? _____

9. What was Goad doing in the third snapshot? _____

10. Air rushes out of Goad this way ←. Draw an arrow to show which way Goad will move. _____

11. Look at the picture below. Goad is filled up with air.

    a. **Make a dotted arrow** from her mouth to show which way the air will move.

    b. **Make a solid arrow** on Goad to show which way she will move.

Skill items

12. Look at object A, object B, and object C. Write two ways that tell how all three objects are the same.

  ① _____

  ② _____

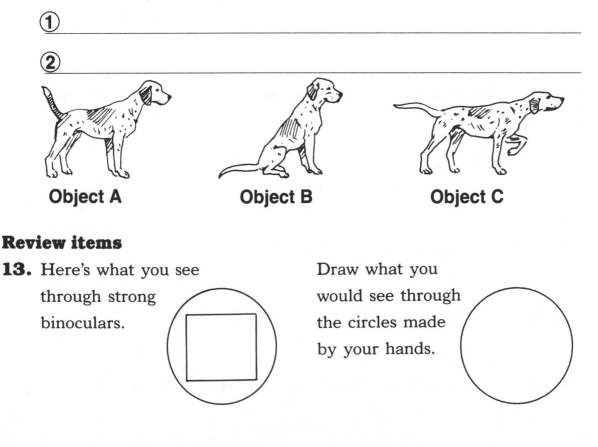

Object A   **Object B**   **Object C**

Review items

13. Here's what you see through strong binoculars.

Draw what you would see through the circles made by your hands.

14. **a.** Write **north, south, east,** and **west** in the right boxes.

    b. Touch the A. An arrow goes from the A. Which direction is that

    arrow going? _____

    c. Make an arrow that goes north from the B.

    d. Make an arrow that goes west from the C.

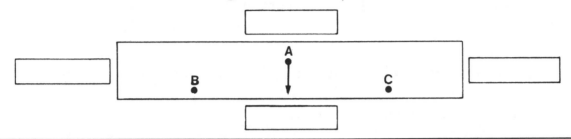

15. The arrow in each picture shows which way the wind is blowing. **Draw the smoke** in each picture.

ERRORS	WA	G	CO	WB	BONUS	T

LESSON 30

A

Story items

1. A boy from New York took three snapshots of Goad getting away from the Browns. What was Goad doing in the first snapshot?

_____

2. What was Goad doing in the second snapshot?

_____

3. What was Goad doing in the third snapshot?

_____

4. Did the Browns' plan work? _____

5. What happened right after the grandmother smiled?

_____

6. Why were so many other people around the lake?

_____

7. Name two things that the people ate at the picnic.

_____

8. Air rushes out of Goad this way ↙ . Draw an arrow to show which

way Goad will move. _____

Skill items

9. Here's a rule: **Moles have legs like shovels.**

    a. A rat is not a mole. So what else do you know about a rat?

    _____

    b. Joe is a mole. So what else do you know about Joe?

    _____

    c. Jan is not a mole. So what else do you know about Jan?

    _____

10. Look at object A, object B, and object C. Write two ways that tell
how all three objects are the same.

    ① _____

    ② _____

      Object A   **Object B**   **Object C**

11. Here are titles for different stories.
- The Man Who Stayed for Dinner
- Ten Exercises
- Mary Buys a Car

a. One story tells about a person who got something new. What's the title of that story?

_____

b. One story tells about a person who wanted to eat. What's the title of that story?

_____

c. One story tells about things you can do to help you be slim and trim. What's the title of that story?

_____

Review items

12. Look at the picture of the balloon.

a. **Make a dotted arrow** to show which way the air will leave the balloon.

b. **Make a solid arrow** on the balloon to show which way it will move.

13. Some things happen as tadpoles grow.

a. **Cross out** what happens first.

b. **Make a box around** what happens last.

- They grow back legs.
- They grow front legs.
- Their tails disappear.

14. a. How many legs does an insect have? _____

b. How many legs does a flea have? _____

c. How many legs does a fly have? _____

d. How many legs does a spider have? _____

15. Look at the picture below.

    a. Write **north, south, east,** and **west** in the right boxes.

    b. An arrow goes from the J. Which direction is that arrow going?

_____

    c. **Make an arrow** that goes west from the K.

    d. Draw the smoke in the picture.

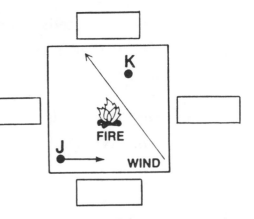

16. What would a fox and a rabbit do when there is a fire?

_____

17. **Underline** the animals that live on the land.

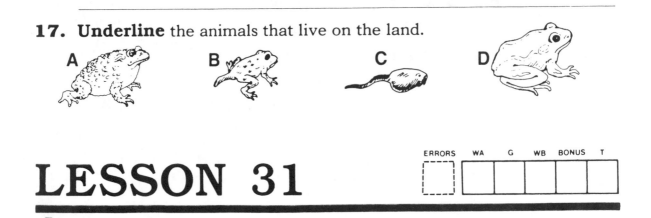

LESSON 31

A

In today's lesson, you read about telling how two things are different.
Use what you learned to do this item.

    1. Look at object A and object B. **Fill in the blanks** to tell how object A is different from object B.

      a. Object A is a square, _____ object B is _____ .

      b. Object A is small, _____ object B is _____ .

      c. Object A is striped, _____ object B is _____ .

 **Object A**    **Object B**

B In today's lesson, you read about toads and warts. Use what you learned to do this item.

2. What did people used to think would happen if your nose touched a

toad? _____

C Story items

3. Finish the sentence. The world is called _____ .

4. What is most of the world covered with? _____

5. Finish the sentence. The land parts of the world are divided into

_____ .

6. What country do you live in? _____

7. Look at the map. Do not use your textbook.

   a. Write **north, south, east,** and **west** in the right boxes.

   b. Make a **U** where the United States is.

   c. Make a **C** where Canada is.

   d. Make an **M** where Mexico is.

   e. Make an **S** where South America is.

Review items

8. How many centimeters are in a meter? _____

9. Look at the lines in the box below.

   a. Write **1** next to each line that is one centimeter long.

   b. Write **2** next to each line that is two centimeters long.

10. Here's what you see through strong binoculars.

Draw what you would see through the circles made by your hands.

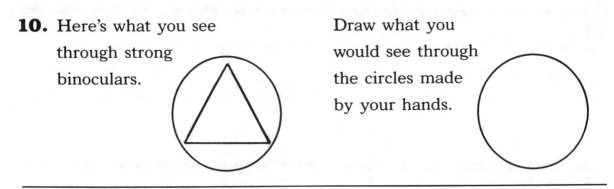

---

11. Look at the picture. The dotted arrow shows which way the air will leave the jet engine. Make a solid arrow on the engine to show which way it will move.

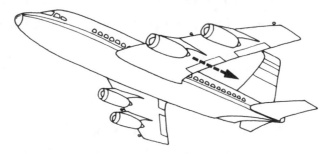

12. a. How many legs does an insect have? _____

    b. How many legs does a flea have? _____

    c. How many legs does a fly have? _____

    d. How many legs does a spider have? _____

13. Circle the animals that live on the land.

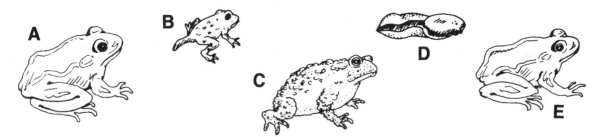

14. Some things happen as tadpoles grow.
    a. Underline what happens first.
    b. Circle what happens last.
- Their tails disappear.
- They grow back legs.
- They grow front legs.

15. **Make a box around** the moles in the picture below.

16. What would a fox and a rabbit do when there is a fire? _____

_____

LESSON 32

A

In today's lesson, you read about telling how two things are different. Use what you learned to do this item.

1. Look at object A and object B. Write three ways that tell how object A is different from object B.

   a. Object A is a circle, _____ object B is _____.

   b. Object A is checked, _____ object B is _____.

   c. Object A is big, _____ object B is _____.

Object A   **Object B**

B

In today's lesson, you read about growing up. Use what you learned to do these items.

2. Which grow up faster, girls or boys? _____

3. Which grow up faster, dogs or mice? _____

4. Jan is a girl that is two years old. Is Jan full grown? _____

5. Spot is a dog that is two years old. Is Spot full grown? _____

6. Pete is a boy that is two years old. Is Pete full grown? _____

C

Story items

7. Name two things that Nancy would do to get her own way.

①_____

②_____

8. Why didn't Nancy want to be a big girl? _____

_____

9. How did Nancy find out that she **was** getting bigger? _____

_____

10. What did Nancy find on her bed? _____

11. The voice told the words to say if you want to stay small. Write those words. _____

_____

12. a. Who could do tricks that Nancy couldn't do? _____

b. How did that make Nancy feel? _____

c. Nancy said, "I can do something you can't do." What did she say

she could do? _____

13. Did Nancy really think that the words would make her small? _____

Review items

14. Look at the map below. Do not use your textbook.

    a. Write **north, south, east,** and **west** in the right boxes.

    b. Make a **J** where the United States is.

    c. Make a **P** where Canada is.

    d. Make an **R** where Mexico is.

    e. Make an **L** where South America is.

15. a. Finish the sentence. The world is called _____.

    b. What is most of the world covered with? _____

16. a. Finish the sentence. The land parts of the world are divided

    into _____.

    b. What country do you live in? _____

LESSON 33

ERRORS	WA	G	WB	BONUS	T

A

In today's lesson you read about ants. Use what you learned to do these items.

    1. How many legs does an insect have? _____

2. How many legs does an ant have? _____

3. How many legs does a fly have? _____

4. How many legs does a flea have? _____

5. Finish the sentence. If an ant weighed as much as a beagle, the

ant could carry an object as heavy as _____.

6. How many ants would it take to weigh as much as a peanut? _____

B

Story items

7. Here's the rule: **If you say the words that are on the record, you will become smaller than a fly.**

a. Did Nancy say the words on the record? _____

b. Write the words Nancy said. _____

_____

c. So what happened to Nancy? _____

_____

8. Why did Nancy think that the jump rope got bigger? _____

_____

9. How big did the ant seem to Nancy? _____

10. Why did Nancy's voice sound like a little squeak?

_____

11. Who gave the record to Nancy? _____

12. Why did he give her the record? _____

_____

Skill items

13. Look at object A and object B. Write two ways that tell how object A is different from object B.

① _____

② _____

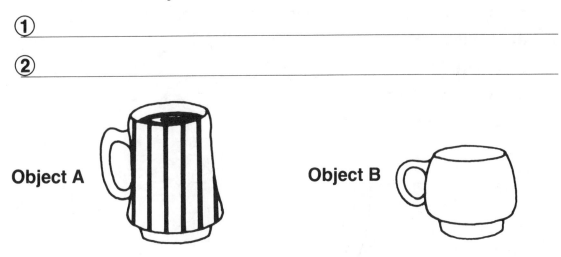

Object A   **Object B**

14. Here's a rule: **All the green men are small.**

    a. Lee is a green man. So what else do you know about Lee?

    _____

    b. Jack is not a green man. So what else do you know about Jack?

    _____

    c. Fred is not a green man. So what else do you know about Fred?

    _____

Review items

15. Some lines in the box below are 1 centimeter long. Write **1 centimeter** over each line that is 1 centimeter long.

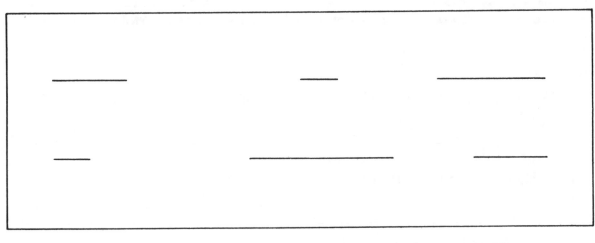

16. Look at the map below. Do not use your textbook.

    a. Write **north, south, east,** and **west** in the right boxes.

    b. Make a **U** where the United States is.

    c. Make a **C** where Canada is.

    d. Make an **M** where Mexico is.

    e. Make an **S** where South America is.

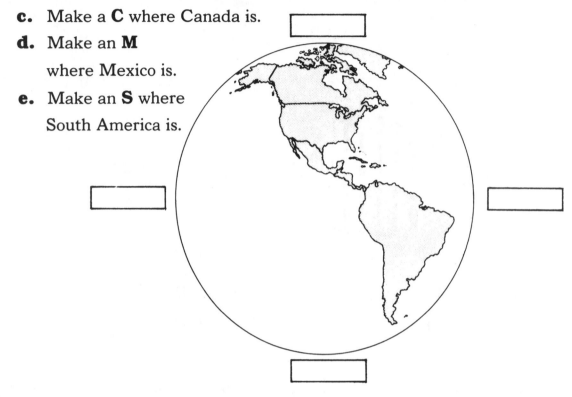

17. What did people used to think would happen if your toe touched a

toad? _____

18. a. Which grow up faster, dogs or mice? _____

    b. Which grow up faster, girls or boys? _____

LESSON 34

ERRORS	WA	G	WB	BONUS	T

A
Story items

    1. Why couldn't Nancy turn on the TV set? _____

_____

    2. Where was the bed that Nancy napped in? _____

_____

3. Whose voices did Nancy hear when she woke up from her nap?

_____

4. Why was Nancy's mother crying? _____

_____

5. Sally told Nancy's mother what happened to Nancy. Did Nancy's

mother believe the story? _____

6. Nancy shouted at her mother. Why couldn't her mother hear Nancy?

_____

7. Here's a rule: **If you get smaller, your voice gets higher.**

   a. Circle the picture that shows when Nancy's voice would be
      highest.

   b. Cross out the picture that shows when Nancy's voice would be
      lowest.

   c. Look at object A and object E. Write one way that tells how both

      objects are the same. _____

A   B   C   D   E

Skill items

8. Look at object A and object B. Write two ways that tell how object A
   is different from object B.

   ① _____

   ② _____

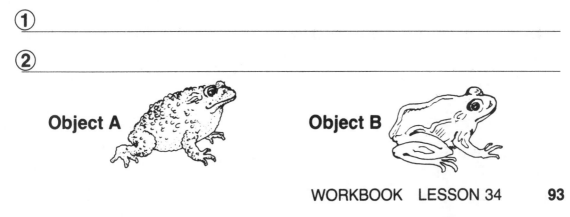

Object A   **Object B**

Review items

9. **Finish the sentence.** If an ant weighed as much as a poodle, the

ant could carry an object as heavy as _____.

10. Look at the picture below.

    a. Write **north, south, east,** and **west** in the right boxes.

    b. An arrow goes from the P. Which direction is that arrow going?

    _____

    c. **Make an arrow** that goes south from the L.

    d. **Draw the smoke** in the picture.

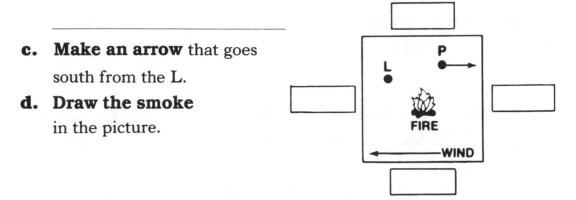

11. Draw an arrow at A and an arrow at B to show which way the string will move when the toad moves the blue fly.

12. Look at the picture. Goad is filled up with air.

    a. **Make a dotted arrow** from her mouth to show which way the air will move.

    b. **Make a solid arrow** on Goad to show which way she will move.

13. Tell how many legs each thing has.

    a. fly _____   **d.** ant _____

    b. insect _____   **e.** flea _____

    c. spider _____

14. Look at the picture.

    a. **Circle** the balloon that lets the most light come through.

    b. **Cross out** the balloon that lets the least light come through.

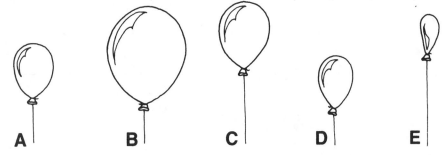

15. Some people in the picture are holding sticks that are 1 meter long.

    Write **1 meter** under each stick that is 1 meter long.

LESSON 35

ERRORS	WA	G	CO	WB	BONUS	T

A

Story items

  1. a. **Finish the rule.** If you get smaller, your voice _____.

     b. Fran got smaller. So what do you know about Fran?

_____

  2. a. **Circle** the ruler that will make the highest sound.

     b. **Cross out** the ruler that will make the lowest sound.

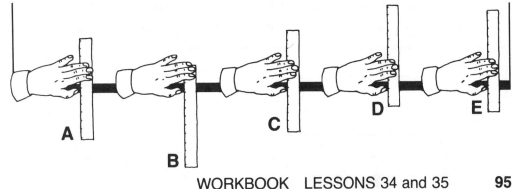

Skill items

3. Look at object A and object B. Write two ways that tell how object A is different from object B.

① _____

② _____

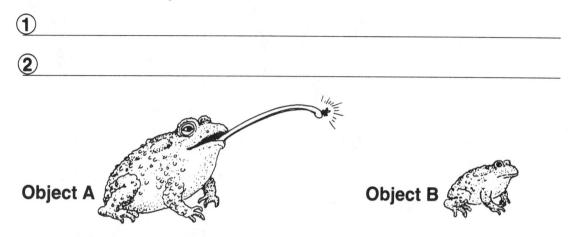

Object A   **Object B**

4. Here are titles for different stories.

  • The Pink Flea   • Pete Gets a Reward   • The Ant That Waddled

  a. One story tells about an insect that was a strange color. What's the title of that story?

  _____

  b. One story tells about an insect that walked like a duck. What's the title of that story?

  _____

  c. One story tells about someone who got something for doing a good job. What's the title of that story?

  _____

Review items

5. Look at the lines in the box below.

  a. Write **1** on each line that is 1 centimeter long.

  b. Write **3** on each line that is 3 centimeters long.

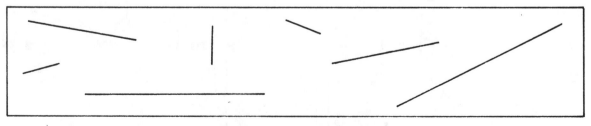

6. Look at the map. Do not use your textbook.

    a. Write **north, south, east,** and **west** in the right boxes.

    b. Make a **B** where the United States is.

    c. Make a **D** where Canada is.

    d. Make an **F** where Mexico is.

    e. Make an **R** where South America is.

7. What did people used to think would happen if your nose touched a

toad? _____

8. Some of the logs below were cut from field trees. **Make a box around** those trees.

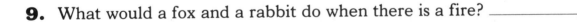

    A   B   C   D   E

9. What would a fox and a rabbit do when there is a fire? _____

_____

10. a. Name one insect that toads eat. _____

    b. **Finish the sentence.** A toad catches insects with its _____.

11. **Circle** the toads in the picture.

  A   B   C   D   E

12. Look at the picture. The man is holding a stick that is one meter long.

a. Write the letter of each object that is one meter long. _____

b. Write the letter of each object that is two meters long. _____

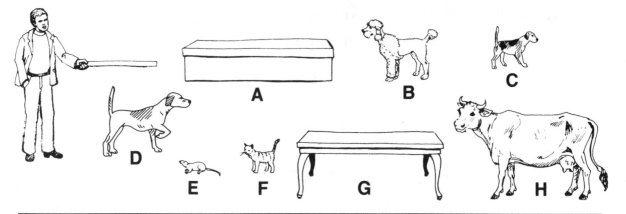

13. Look at the picture of the felt-tipped pen.

a. Write these names on the picture: **shaft**   **felt tip**   **ink**

b. The pen in the picture does not have an eraser. **Make an X** to show where an eraser would go on the pen.

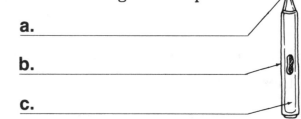

a. _____

b. _____

c. _____

14. Each canoe in the picture below has a hole in the front. One canoe will sink fast. One canoe will sink slowly. One canoe will not sink.

a. Which canoe will sink fast? _____

b. Which canoe will not sink? _____

c. Which canoe will sink slowly? _____

d. Look at object B and object C. Write one way that tells how both objects are the same. _____

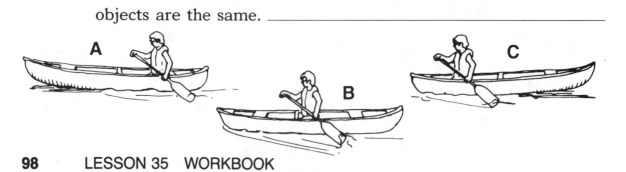

15. Look at the picture below.

    a. Which letter is on the path? _____

    b. Which letter is on the shore of the lake? _____

    c. Which letter is in the forest? _____

    d. Which letter is in the middle of the lake? _____

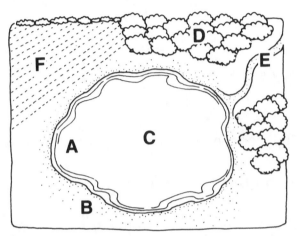

16. Look at the picture below.

    a. Make an arrow **over each canoe** to show which way the canoe is moving.

    b. Make an arrow **under each paddle** to show which way the paddle is moving in the water.

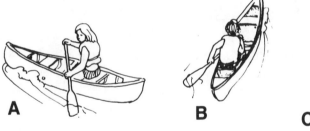

LESSON 36

ERRORS	WA	G	WB	BONUS	T

A

In today's lesson, you read about why sugar shines. Use what you learned to do these items.

1. **Finish the sentence.** If a grain of sugar were very big, it would look like _____.

2. What kind of corners does a grain of sugar have? _____

3. A grain of sugar is no bigger than _____.

B

Story items

4. What did Nancy say to get small? _____

   _____

5. The walk to the bedroom doorway was much longer for Nancy than for her mother and the police officer. Why? _____

   _____

6. Why did Nancy think she would get lost? _____

   _____

7. In this story, Nancy found something to eat.

   a. What did she find? _____

   b. How big was it to Nancy? _____

   c. Why did she sniff it before she started eating it? _____

   _____

   d. How much of it did she eat? _____

   e. Why didn't she eat the whole thing? _____

   _____

8. After Nancy finished eating, she wanted something.

   a. What did she want? _____

   b. Did she know how she was going to get it? _____

9. Circle the picture that could be Nancy standing next to the big crumb she found.

A   B   C   D

10. Write what Nancy has learned about being so small.

_____

_____

Skill items

11. Look at object A and object B.

   a. Write one way that tells how both objects are the same.

   _____

   b. Write two ways that tell how object A is different from object B.

      ① _____

      ② _____

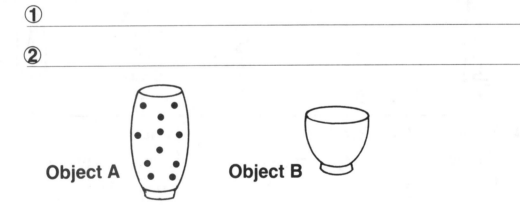

Object A   Object B

Review items

12. How many centimeters are in one meter? _____

13. Some lines in the box below are not one centimeter long. **Cross out** every line that is not one centimeter long.

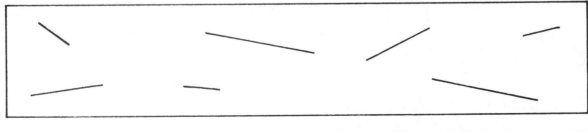

14. Look at the picture below.

    a. Write **north, south, east,** and **west** in the right boxes.

    b. An arrow goes from the P. Which direction is that arrow going?

_____

    c. Make an arrow that goes east from the F.

    d. Draw the smoke in the picture.

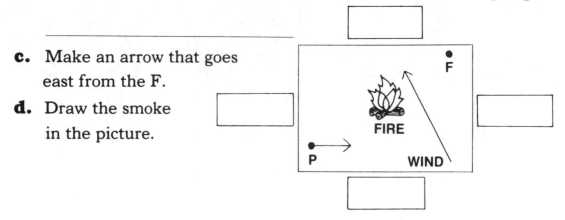

15. Here's the rule: **If you get smaller, your voice gets higher.**

    a. **Circle** the picture that shows when Nancy's voice would be highest.

    b. **Cross out** the picture that shows when Nancy's voice would be lowest.

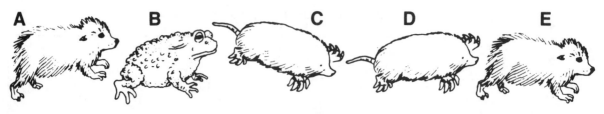

    A   **B**   **C**   **D**   **E**

16. Here's what you see through the circles made by your hands.

Draw what you would see through strong binoculars.

17. **Underline** the moles in the picture below.

  A   **B**   **C**   **D**   **E**

18. What do a mole's legs look like? _____

LESSON 37

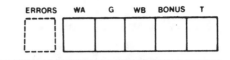

A

In today's lesson you read about water. Use what you learned to do these items.

1. What does water have? _____

2. Look at the picture.
   The dotted line shows how
   much water will go into the tube.
   Draw the skin that covers the top
   of that water.

B

In today's lesson you read about dew. Use what you learned to do these items.

3. You can see drops of water on grass early in the morning. What are

   those drops called? _____

4. Does dew form in the middle of the day? _____

5. **Circle the answer.** Dew forms when the air gets _____

     • warmer   • cooler

C

Story items

6. **Finish the rule.** If tiny animals fall from high places, _____

   _____ .

7. When Nancy was thirsty, she didn't scream and yell and stamp her

   feet. Why not? _____

8. Why wasn't there any dew on the grass? _____

_____

9. Where did Nancy go to look for water? _____

10. Why did Nancy slip on the strip of wood? _____

_____

11. a. How high was the cabinet to Nancy? _____

_____

b. Did Nancy get hurt when she fell? _____

c. Why not? _____

12. These animals fell from a cliff. Circle the words that tell what happened to each animal.

a. ant	**b. mouse**	**c. pointer**	**d. squirrel**	**e. poodle**
wasn't hurt	wasn't hurt	wasn't hurt	wasn't hurt	wasn't hurt
was hurt	was hurt	was hurt	was hurt	was hurt
was killed	was killed	was killed	was killed	was killed

Skill items

13. Here's a rule: **Pointers can run very fast.**

a. A horse is not a pointer. So what else do you know about a horse?

_____

b. Jake is not a pointer. So what else do you know about Jake?

_____

c. Meg is a pointer. So what else do you know about Meg?

_____

14. List the two things that Nancy has learned about being very small.

① _____

② _____

15. Look at object A and object B.

   a. Write one way that tells how both objects are the same.

   _____

   b. Write two ways that tell how object A is different from object B.

   ① _____

   ② _____

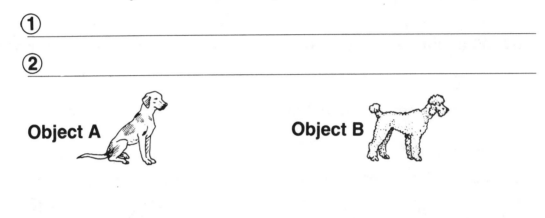

Object A   **Object B**

LESSON 38

ERRORS	WA	G	WB	BONUS	T

A

In today's lesson, you read more about the skin that water has. Use what you learned to do these items.

   1. Some hairs in the picture are being pushed down. Some are being pulled up. Look at the skin around each hair.

      a. Write **up** on every hair that is moving up.

      b. Write **down** on every hair that is moving down.

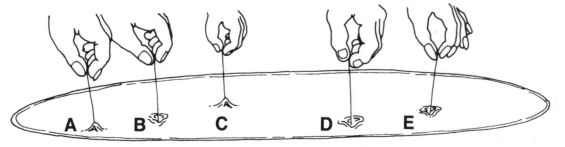

B

Story items

2. How big were the water drops to Nancy? _____

_____

3. When Nancy first touched the water drop, did her hand get wet?

_____

4. What did Nancy have to do to get her hand inside the water drop?

_____

5. What did Nancy have to do to get her head inside the water drop?

_____

6. What happened when Nancy tried to pull her head back out of the

water drop? _____

7. **Circle** the water striders.

8. List the three things that Nancy has learned about being very small.

①_____

_____

②_____

_____

③_____

_____

9. a. Is a water strider an insect? _____

b. How many legs does a water strider have? _____

c. How many legs does an ant have? _____

d. How many legs does a spider have? _____

e. How many legs does a flea have? _____

f. How many legs does a cat have? _____

Skill items

10. Look at object A and object B.

a. Write one way that tells how both objects are the same.

_____

b. Write two ways that tell how object A is different from object B.

① _____

② _____

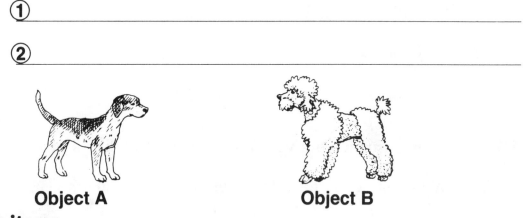

Object A   **Object B**

Review items

11. Finish the rule. If tiny animals fall from high places, _____

_____.

12. These animals fell from an airplane. **Underline** the words that tell what happened to each animal.

a. poodle	**b. squirrel**	**c. mouse**	**d. flea**
wasn't hurt	wasn't hurt	wasn't hurt	wasn't hurt
was hurt	was hurt	was hurt	was hurt
was killed	was killed	was killed	was killed

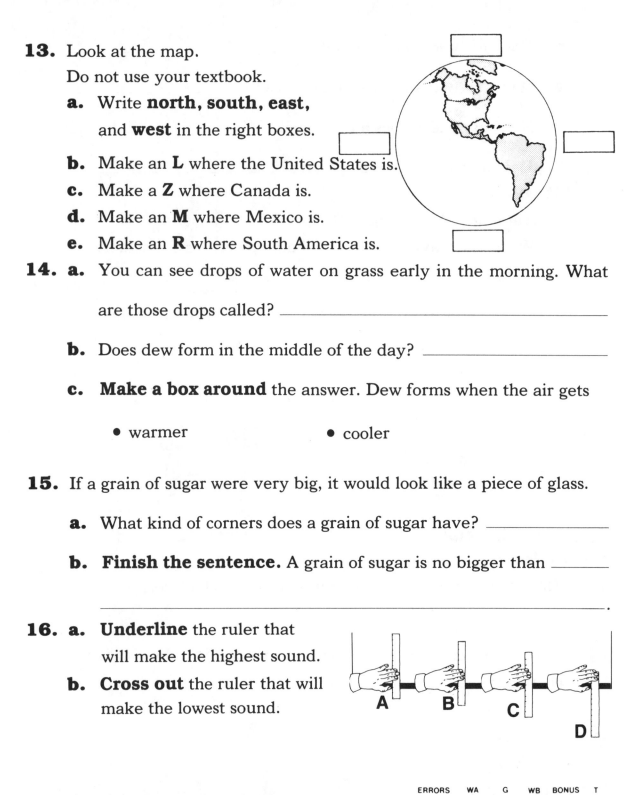

13. Look at the map.

Do not use your textbook.

    a. Write **north, south, east,**

        and **west** in the right boxes.

    b. Make an **L** where the United States is.

    c. Make a **Z** where Canada is.

    d. Make an **M** where Mexico is.

    e. Make an **R** where South America is.

14. a. You can see drops of water on grass early in the morning. What

        are those drops called? _____

    b. Does dew form in the middle of the day? _____

    c. **Make a box around** the answer. Dew forms when the air gets

        • warmer   • cooler

15. If a grain of sugar were very big, it would look like a piece of glass.

    a. What kind of corners does a grain of sugar have? _____

    b. **Finish the sentence.** A grain of sugar is no bigger than _____

    _____.

16. a. **Underline** the ruler that
will make the highest sound.

    b. **Cross out** the ruler that will
make the lowest sound.

LESSON 39

A

In today's lesson you read about grams. Use what you learned to do these
items.

1. Finish the sentence. When we weigh very small things, we use

_____ .

2. Some things in the picture weigh 1 gram. Some weigh 2 grams. Some weigh 5 grams. Fill in the blanks to tell how much each object weighs.

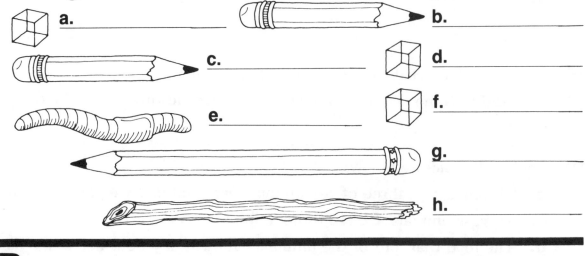

a. _____   **b.** _____

c. _____   **d.** _____

e. _____   **f.** _____

g. _____

h. _____

B In today's lesson, you read about comparing things. Use what you learned to do this item.

3. Look at object A and object B below. Compare the objects.

   a. Tell a way the objects are the same. _____

   _____

   b. Tell a way the objects are different. _____

   _____

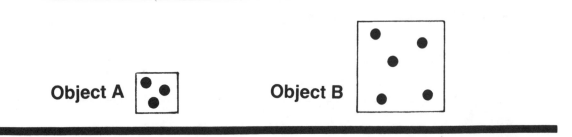

Object A   Object B

C

Story items

   4. Finish the rule. The food that very small animals eat each day

may weigh _____ .

5. Are you a small animal? _____

6. Does the food that you eat each day weigh as much as you do? _____

7. a. How many times did Nancy wake up during the night? _____

b. Why did she wake up? _____

_____

8. What did Nancy eat the first time she woke up? _____

9. Why didn't Nancy eat a cookie crumb the second time she woke up?

_____

10. Look at the picture below.

a. The food that three of the animals eat each day weighs as much as those animals. **Circle** those animals.

b. The food that four of the animals eat each day does not weigh as much as those animals. **Cross out** those animals.

11. You know four things that Nancy has learned about being very small. List three of those things.

① _____

_____

② _____

_____

③ _____

_____

Review items

12. Look at the lines in the box below.

  a. Write **1** next to each line that is 1 centimeter long.

  b. Write **3** next to each line that is 3 centimeters long.

13. Cross out the water striders in the picture below.

14. Some hairs in the picture are being pushed down. Some are being pulled up. Look at the skin next to each hair.

  a. Write **up** on every hair that is moving up.

  b. Write **down** on every hair that is moving down.

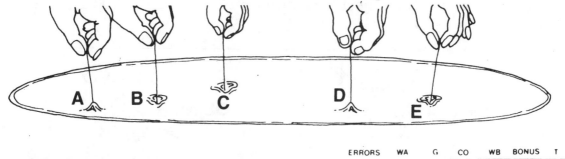

LESSON 40

ERRORS   WA   G   CO   WB   BONUS   T

A

In today's lesson, you read about grams. Use what you learned to do these items.

  1. Does a housefly weigh **more than a gram** or **less than a gram?**

  _____

  2. Does a glass of water weigh **more than a gram** or **less than a gram?** _____

  3. How many ants would it take to weigh one gram? _____

Look at the scale in the picture.

a. How many grams are on the left side of the scale?_____

b. So how much weight is on the side of the scale with the water

striders? _____

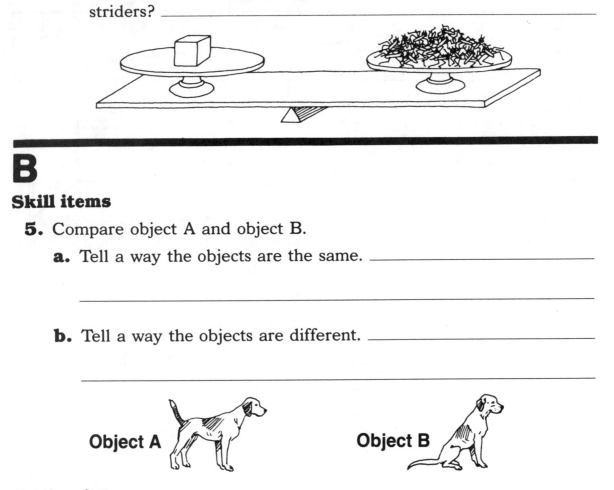

B

Skill items

5. Compare object A and object B.

a. Tell a way the objects are the same. _____

_____

b. Tell a way the objects are different. _____

_____

Object A   **Object B**

Review items

6. Finish the sentence. When we weigh very small things, we use

_____.

7. Some things in the picture weigh 1 gram. Some weigh 2 grams. Some weigh 5 grams. Fill in the blanks to tell how much each object weighs.

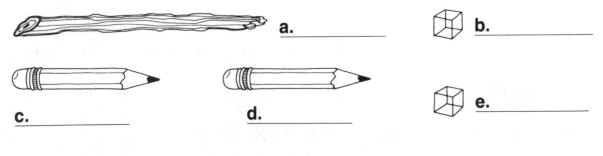

a. _____   **b.** _____

c. _____   **d.** _____   **e.** _____

8. Tell how many legs each thing has.

    a. ant _____   **d.** man _____

    b. insect _____   **e.** fly _____

    c. spider _____   **f.** water strider _____

9. Look at the picture below.

    a. The food that three of the animals eat each day weighs as much as those animals. **Underline** those animals.

    b. The food that four of the animals eat each day does not weigh as much as those animals. **Circle** those animals.

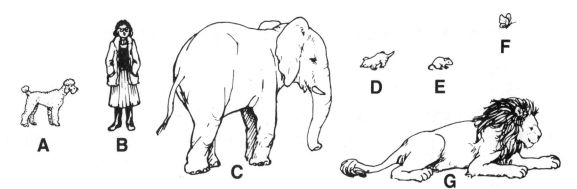

10. Look at the lines in the box below.

    a. Write **1** on each line that is 1 centimeter long.

    b. Write **3** on each line that is 3 centimeters long.

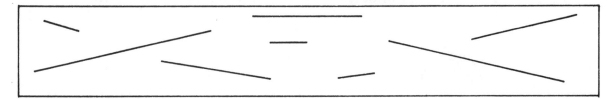

11. a. Make a box around the ruler that will make the highest sound.

    b. Underline the ruler that will make the lowest sound.

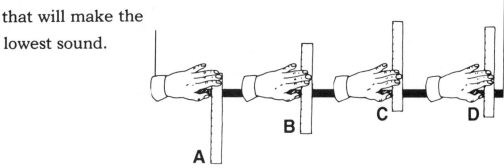

a. Finish the sentence. If an ant weighed as much as a horse, the ant could carry an object as heavy as _____.

b. How many ants would it take to weigh as much as a peanut?

_____

13. a. Which grow up faster, girls or boys? _____

b. Which grow up faster, dogs or mice? _____

14. a. Finish the sentence. The world is called _____.

b. What is most of the world covered with? _____

15. a. Finish the sentence. The land parts of the world are divided into _____.

b. What country do you live in? _____

16. What did people use   to think would happen if your hand touched a toad? _____

17. Look at the picture below.

a. Underline the balloon that lets the most light come through.

b. Cross out the balloon that lets the least light come through.

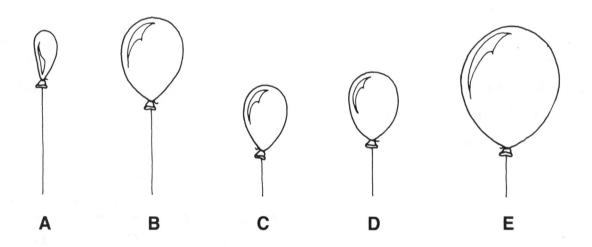

A   B   C   D   E

LESSON 41

A

Story items

1. Why couldn't Nancy see very well when she walked to the kitchen?

_____

2. Why didn't Nancy act like a baby when she was very hungry? _____

_____

3. a. Was Nancy frightened when she climbed the kitchen counter? _____

b. Why not? _____

4. What did Nancy smell on the kitchen counter? _____

5. a. How many pieces of toast were on the plate? _____

b. What did that pile look like to Nancy? _____

_____

6. a. Did Nancy have to climb the pile of toast to get something to

eat? _____

b. Why not? _____

_____

7. How many toast crumbs did Nancy eat? _____

8. Nancy hated toast when she was full-sized. Why doesn't she hate

toast now? _____

_____

9. a. How much does Nancy weigh? _____

b. Nancy ate a lot of food in one day. How much did that food

weigh? _____

10. You know four things that Nancy has learned about being small. List three of those things.

① _____

_____

② _____

_____

③ _____

_____

Skill items

11. Compare object A and object B. First tell how they are the same. Then tell how they are different.

_____

_____

_____

Object A  **Object B**

Review items

12. a. Finish the sentence. When we weigh very small things,

we use _____.

b. Some things in the picture below weigh 1 gram. Some weigh 2 grams. Some weigh 5 grams. Fill in the blanks to tell how much each object weighs.

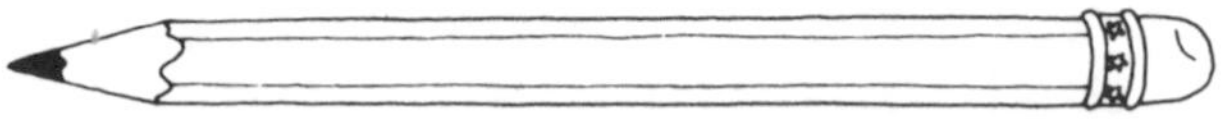

a. _____

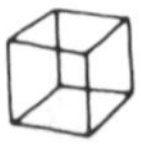

b. _____   c. _____

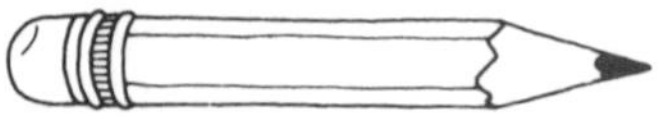

d. _____

e. _____   f. _____

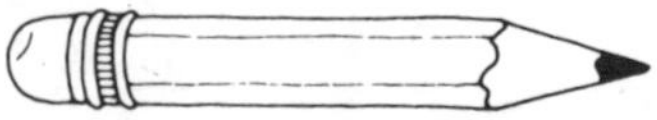

g. _____   h. _____

13. Look at the scale in the picture.

    a. How many grams are on the left side of the scale? _____

    b. How many fleas are on the other side? _____

    c. So how much weight is on the side of the scale with the fleas?

_____

14. a. Finish the sentence. The world is called _____ .

    b. What is most of the world covered with? _____

LESSON 42

ERRORS	WA	G	WB	BONUS	T

A

Story items

  1. a. Was Nancy afraid to jump down from the counter top? _____

    b. Did she get hurt when she jumped? _____

    c. Tell why. _____

2. Who woke Nancy? _____

3. Was Nancy happy about being so little? _____

4. Did Nancy change her mind about growing up? _____

5. What did Nancy learn about acting like a baby? _____

_____

6. You know four things that Nancy has learned about being very small. Write three of those things.

  ① _____

_____

② _____

_____

③ _____

_____

Skill items

7. Compare object A and object B. First tell how they are the same. Then tell how they are different.

_____

_____

_____

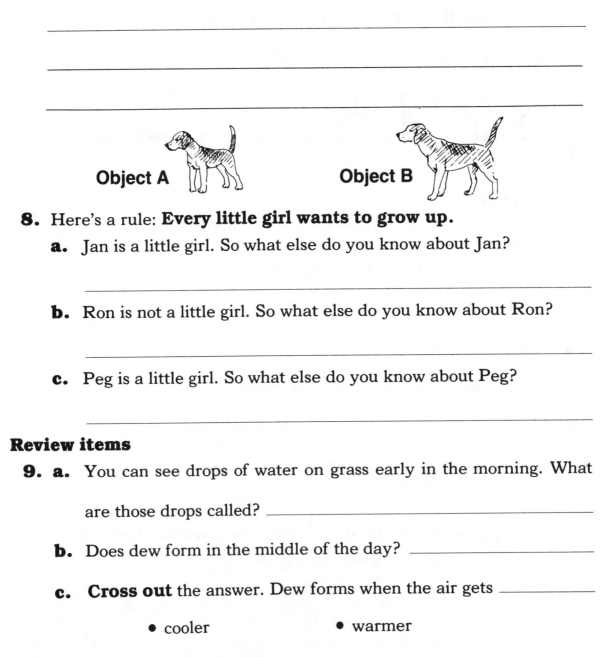

Object A   **Object B**

8. Here's a rule: **Every little girl wants to grow up.**

   a. Jan is a little girl. So what else do you know about Jan?

   _____

   b. Ron is not a little girl. So what else do you know about Ron?

   _____

   c. Peg is a little girl. So what else do you know about Peg?

   _____

Review items

9. a. You can see drops of water on grass early in the morning. What

   are those drops called? _____

   b. Does dew form in the middle of the day? _____

   c. **Cross out** the answer. Dew forms when the air gets _____

         • cooler   • warmer

10. a. Does a housefly weigh **more than a gram** or **less than a gram?** _____

b. Does a long pencil weigh **more than a gram** or **less than a gram?** _____

11. Look at the picture. The dotted line shows how much water will go into the tube. **Draw** the skin that covers the top of that water.

12. Look at the picture below.

a. Which letter is on the shore of the lake? _____

b. Which letter is in the forest? _____

c. Which letter is in the middle of the lake? _____

d. Which letter is on the path? _____

13. Look at the map. Do not use your textbook.

a. Write **north, south, east,** and **west** in the right boxes.

b. Make a **Z** where the United States is.

c. Make an **X** where Canada is.

d. Make an **F** where Mexico is.

e. Make a **D** where South America is.

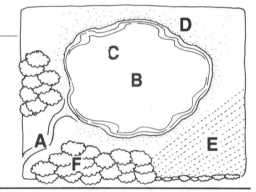

14. What do a mole's legs look like? _____

15. Look at the picture. The man is holding a stick that is one meter long.

  a. Write the letter of each object that is one meter long. _____

  b. Write the letter of each object that is two meters long. _____

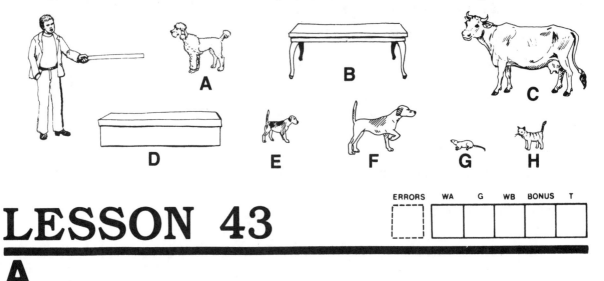

ERRORS WA G WB BONUS T

LESSON 43

A

In today's lesson, you read about miles. Use what you learned to do these items.

1. Look at the map.

  • Things that are this far apart on the map ⟷ are 1 mile apart.

  • Things that are this far apart ⟵————⟶ are 2 miles apart.

  a. Write **1** in the circle if the line stands for 1 mile.

  b. Write **2** in the circle if the line stands for 2 miles.

  c. How far is it from the school to the lake? _____

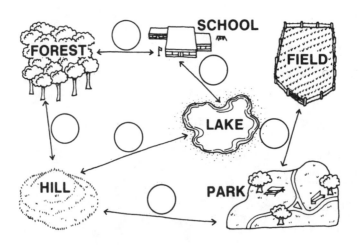

2. How many meters are in one mile? _____

B

Story items

3. Why was Nancy crying? _____

_____

4. Nancy told about two things to prove that she had been very small. Name those two things.

① _____

② _____

5. Does Nancy want to be called a baby now? _____

6. How does Nancy feel now about growing up? _____

7. What does Nancy tell herself when things go wrong? _____

_____

8. a. One of these pictures shows Nancy when she was very small.

Which picture is that? _____

b. How do you know? _____

_____

A   B   C

Skill items

9. Compare object A and object B. First tell how they are the same. Then tell how they are different.

_____

_____

_____

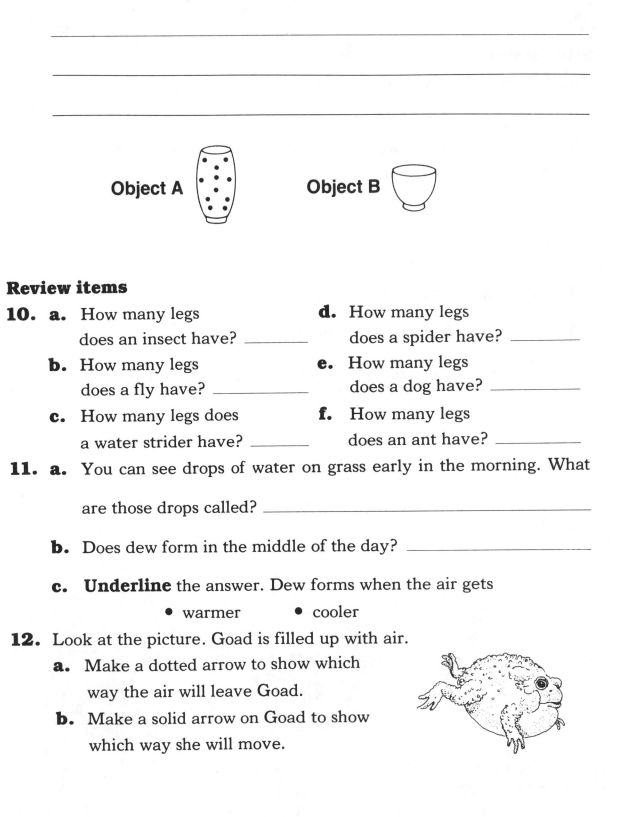

Object A   **Object B**

Review items

10. a. How many legs
does an insect have? _____

b. How many legs
does a fly have? _____

c. How many legs does
a water strider have? _____

d. How many legs
does a spider have? _____

e. How many legs
does a dog have? _____

f. How many legs
does an ant have? _____

11. a. You can see drops of water on grass early in the morning. What

are those drops called? _____

b. Does dew form in the middle of the day? _____

c. **Underline** the answer. Dew forms when the air gets

• warmer   • cooler

12. Look at the picture. Goad is filled up with air.

a. Make a dotted arrow to show which
way the air will leave Goad.

b. Make a solid arrow on Goad to show
which way she will move.

13. Here's what you see through strong binoculars.  Draw what you would see through the circles made by your hands.

14. Look at the picture below.

    a. Write **north, south, east,** and **west** in the right boxes.

    b. An arrow goes from the L. Which direction is that arrow going?

_____

    c. Make an arrow that goes south from the Q.

    d. Draw the smoke in the picture.

WIND

FIRE

L

Q

LESSON 44

A

In today's lesson, you read about miles. Use what you learned to do these items.

    1. How many meters are in one mile? _____

    2. Look at the map below.

        a. What part of the world is shown on the map? _____

        b. The map shows how far apart some places are. One line shows 13 hundred miles. The other line shows 25 hundred miles.

        How far is it from **A** to **B?**

        _____

        c. How far is it from **C** to **D?**

        _____

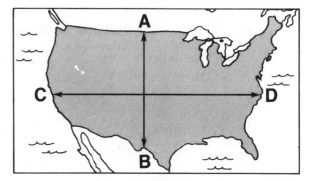

B

Story items

3. Finish the rule. When something moves in one direction, _____

_____ .

4. a. Make a dotted arrow to show which way the air will leave the balloon.

   b. Make a solid arrow on the balloon to show which way it will move.

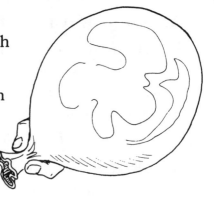

5. Look at the picture below.

   a. Make an arrow **over** each canoe to show which way the canoe is moving.

   b. Make an arrow **under** each paddle to show which way the paddle is moving in the water.

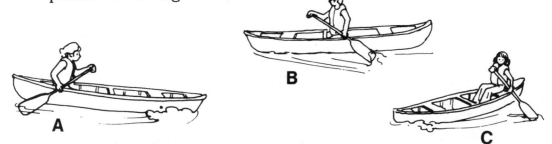

6. Look at the picture below. Goad is filled up with air.

   a. Make a dotted arrow from her mouth to show which way the air will move.

   b. Make a solid arrow on Goad to show which way she will move.

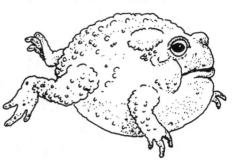

7. The dotted arrow shows which way the boy will jump. **Make a solid arrow** on the block of ice to show which way it will move.

8. The dotted arrow shows which way the girl will jump. **Make a solid arrow** on the back of the boat to show which way it will move.

Review items

9. a. Name one insect that toads eat. _____

b. **Finish the sentence.** A toad catches insects with its _____

10. **Draw a box around** the moles in the picture below.

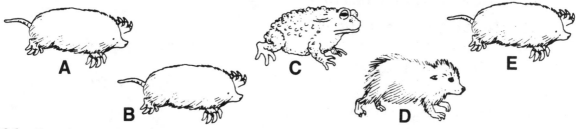

11. Look at the map.

- Things that are this far apart on the map ⟷ are 2 miles apart.

- Things that are this far apart ⟵——⟶ are 4 miles apart.

a. Write **2** in the circle if the line stands for 2 miles.

b. Write **4** in the circle if the line stands for 4 miles.

c. How far is it from the airport to the park?

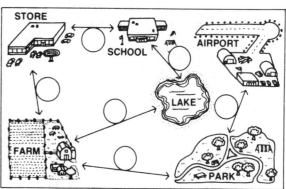

_____

12. How many meters are in one mile? _____

13. Look at the picture below. The dotted line shows how much water will go into the tube. **Draw the skin** that covers the top of that water.

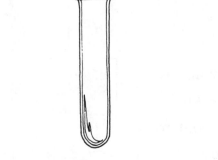

14. Draw an arrow at A and an arrow at B to show which way the string will move when the toad moves the blue fly.

15. Some things happen as tadpoles grow.

    a. **Circle** what happens first.

    b. **Underline** what happens last.

      • Their tail disappears.

      • They grow back legs.

      • They grow front legs.

16. Look at the picture below.

    a. Write **north, south, east,** and **west** in the right boxes.

    b. An arrow goes from the J. Which direction is that arrow going?

    _____

    c. Make an arrow that goes south from the P.

    d. **Draw the smoke** in the picture.

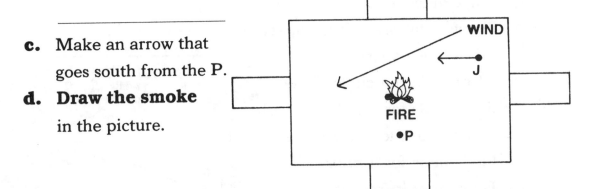

17. Some lines in the box below are one centimeter long **Cross out** the lines that are one centimeter long.

LESSON 45

A

Story items

1. Finish the rule. When something moves in one direction, _____

_____ .

2. a. Make a dotted arrow from a jet engine to show which way the air will move.

   b. Make a solid arrow on the engine to show which way it will move.

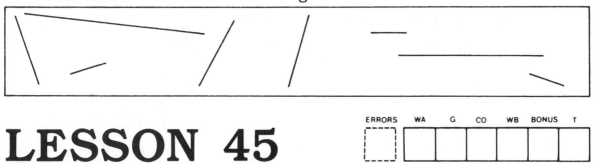

3. The dotted arrow shows which way the bullet will leave the gun. Make a solid arrow on the gun to show which way it will move.

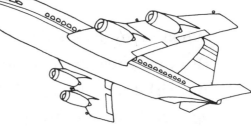

4. Look at the picture below.

   a. Make an arrow **over** each canoe to show which way the canoe is moving.

   b. Make an arrow **under** each paddle to show which way the paddle is moving in the water.

A   B   C

5. **a.** Make a dotted arrow to show which way the air will leave the balloon.

    b. Make a solid arrow on the balloon to show which way it will move.

6. Look at the picture. Goad is filled up with air.

    a. Make a dotted arrow from her mouth to show which way the air will move.

    b. Make a solid arrow on Goad to show which way she will move.

7. When a boy jumps this way ↖, there is a push against the ground. Draw an arrow to show the direction of that push. _____

8. If a girl dove into a pool in this direction ↗, there would be a push against the side of the pool. Draw an arrow to show the direction of that push. _____

Skill items

9. Compare object A and object B. First tell how they are the same. Then tell how they are different.

_____

_____

_____

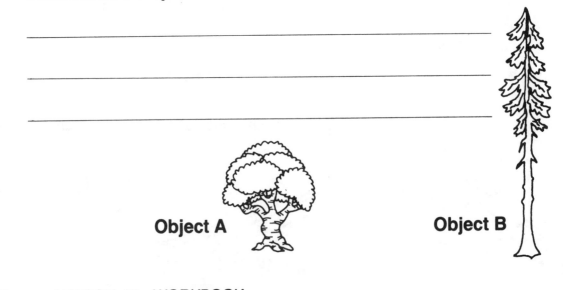

Object A   **Object B**

Review items

10. Look at the map.

- Things that are this far apart on the map $\longleftrightarrow$ are 5 miles apart.

- Things that are this far apart $\longleftrightarrow$ are 10 miles apart.

a. Write **5** in the circle if the line stands for 5 miles.

b. Write **10** in the circle if the line stands for 10 miles.

c. How far is it from the forest to the police station?

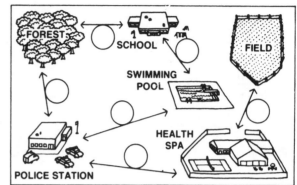

_____

11. Some lines in the box below are 1 centimeter long. Write **1 centimeter** next to each of those lines.

12. Draw an arrow at A and an arrow at B to show which way the string will move when the toad moves the blue fly.

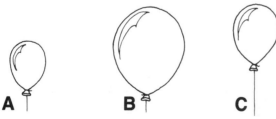

13. Look at the picture below.

a. **Circle** the balloon that lets the most light come through.

b. **Cross out** the balloon that lets the least light come through.

14. **Cross out** the toads in the picture.

A   B   C   D

15. Everybody in the picture below should be on a diet. Write what kind of diet each person should be on.

- Write **L** for a diet **to lose weight.**
- Write **P** for a diet **to put on weight.**
- Write **H** for a diet **to stay healthy.**

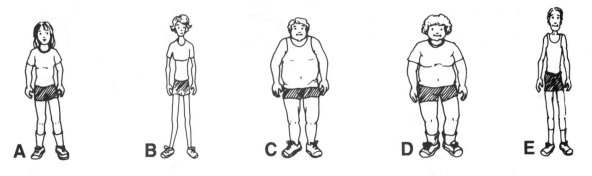

16. Some people in the picture are holding sticks that are 1 meter long. Write **1 meter** under each stick that is 1 meter long.

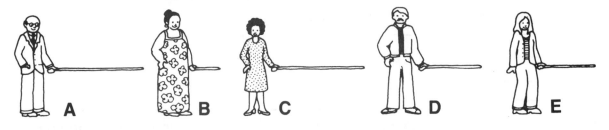

17. Look at the map below.

a. What part of the world is shown on the map? _____

b. The map shows how far apart some places are. One line shows 13 hundred miles. The other line shows 25 hundred miles.

How far is it from **F** to **G**? _____

c. How far is it from **K** to **L**? _____

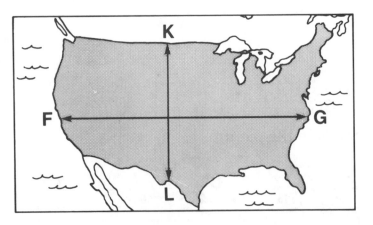

LESSON 46

A In today's lesson, you read about miles per hour. Use what you learned to do these items.

1. Finish the sentence. When we talk about miles per hour, we tell

how _____ something is moving.

2. Look at the picture below.

   a. How fast is truck **A** going? _____

   b. How fast is truck **B** going? _____

   c. Which truck is going faster? _____

   d. How fast is boy **C** going? _____

   e. How fast is boy **D** going? _____

   f. Which boy is going faster? _____

A	B	C	D
55	40	4	6

B

Story items

3. Where was Herman born? _____

4. Who has more brothers and sisters, you or Herman? _____

5. Finish the rule. When flies are born, they are worms called _____ .

6. Finish the sentence. Herman was a maggot for _____ .

7. Flies are insects. So how many legs does Herman have? _____

8. Do flies change size on the inside? _____

9. Do flies change size on the outside? _____

10. Name three things that flies love to do. ① _____

② _____ ③ _____

11. What makes Herman different from any other fly? _____

_____

12. Circle the picture that shows how Herman looked when he came out
of the egg.

13. a. Cross out the youngest fly.

   b. Draw a box around the oldest fly.

Skill items

14. Compare object A and object B. Remember what you're going to tell
first and what you're going to tell next.

_____

_____

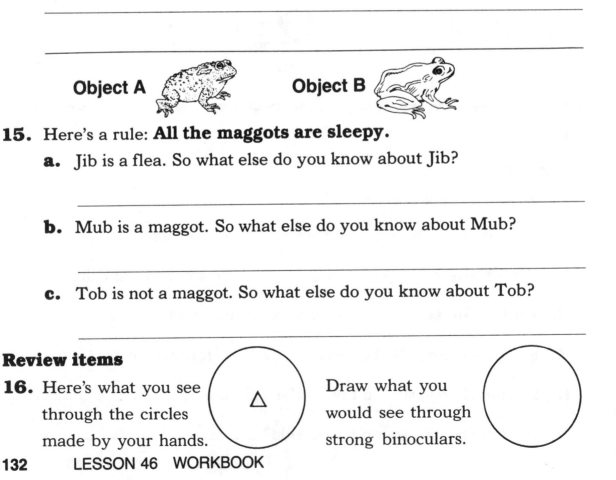

Object A   **Object B**

15. Here's a rule: **All the maggots are sleepy.**

   a. Jib is a flea. So what else do you know about Jib?

   _____

   b. Mub is a maggot. So what else do you know about Mub?

   _____

   c. Tob is not a maggot. So what else do you know about Tob?

   _____

Review items

16. Here's what you see
through the circles
made by your hands.

△

Draw what you
would see through
strong binoculars.

17. The dotted arrow shows which way the boy will jump. **Make a solid arrow** on the block of ice to show which way it will move.

18. Look at the map.

    a. What part of the world is shown on the map? _____

    b. The map shows how far apart some places are. One line shows 13 hundred miles. The other line shows 25 hundred miles.

    How far is it from **S** to **T**?

    _____

    c. How far is it from **G** to **H**?

    _____

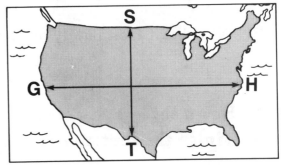

LESSON 47

ERRORS	WA	G	WB	BONUS	T

A In today's lesson, you read about miles per hour. Use what you learned to do these items.

  1. Fill in the blank. The _____ inside a car tells how fast the car is moving.

  2. Each speedometer in the picture shows how fast the car is moving.

    a. How fast is car **A** going? _____

    b. How fast is car **B** going? _____

    c. Which car is going faster? _____

B

Story items

3. What city was Herman born in? _____

4. What airport was close to where Herman was born? _____

5. How far was the airport from where Herman was born? _____

6. Finish the rule. The faster the cab moves, the faster _____

_____ .

7. Why didn't Herman fly off the cab? _____

_____

8. How many legs does Herman have? _____

9. Finish the sentence. The two women were part of the crew of a

_____ .

10. Why did Herman fly into the woman's purse? _____

_____

11. Name two things that Herman liked about the cab.

①_____   ②_____

12. Look at the pictures.

a. One picture shows Herman when the cab is standing still. Which

picture is that? _____

b. One picture shows Herman when the cab is going 40 miles

per hour. Which picture is that? _____

13. a. Underline the thing that Herman rode on to the airport.

   b. Make an **X** on that thing to show where Herman was when he
   rode to the airport.

A B C D

Review items

14. Look at the picture below.

   a. How fast is truck **R** going? _____

   b. How fast is truck **S** going? _____

   c. Which truck is going faster? _____

R 25

S 30

15. Finish the sentence. When flies are born, they are worms called

_____.

16. a. How many legs
   does an insect have? _____

   b. How many legs
   does a fly have? _____

   c. How many legs
   does a cat have? _____

   d. How many legs
   does a flea have? _____

   e. How many legs does
   a water strider have? _____

   f. How many legs does
   a spider have? _____

17. a. Circle the youngest fly.   **b. Underline** the oldest fly.

A   B   C   D

LESSON 48

A In today's lesson, you read about airplane crew members. Use what you learned to do these items.

1. Look at the cut-away picture of an airplane.

   a. **Circle** each flight attendant.

   b. **Cross out** the pilot.

B In today's lesson, you read facts about speed.

2. Here's how fast different things can go: **20 miles per hour**

                                                35 miles per hour

                                2 hundred miles per hour

                                5 hundred miles per hour

   a. Which speed tells how fast a jet can fly?

_____

   b. Which speed tells how fast a pointer can run?

_____

   c. Which speed tells how fast a fast man can run?

_____

C

Story items

3. How far is it from New York City to San Francisco? _____

4. Look at the map.

   a. Make an **X** where New York City is.

   b. Make a **Y** where San Francisco is.

136   LESSON 48 WORKBOOK

5. Why did Herman fly into the woman's purse? _____

_____

6. Why didn't Herman want to stay in the purse? _____

_____

7. a. Herman tried to take a nap on something. What was it? _____

_____

b. Why did that place feel great to Herman? _____

c. What object did a passenger drop on that place? _____

8. How many passengers were on the jumbo jet? _____

9. **Circle** the plane that Herman was in.

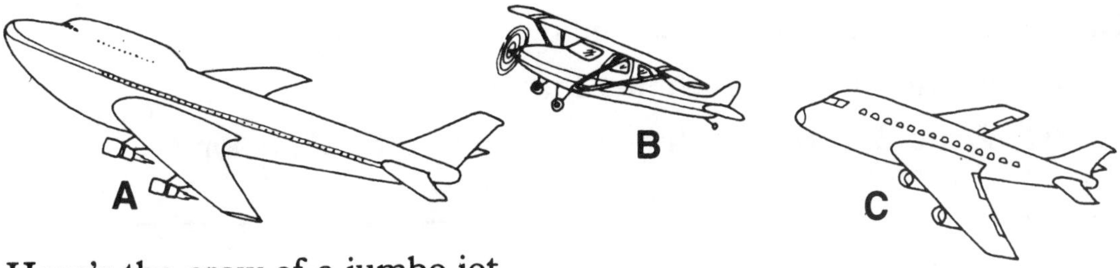

A   B   C

10. Here's the crew of a jumbo jet.

a. **Circle** the crew member who brought Herman on board.

b. **Make an X** to show where Herman was.

A   B   C   D

Review items

11. Fill in the blank. The _____ inside a car tells how fast the car is moving.

12. Each speedometer in the picture shows how fast the car is moving.

   a. How fast is car **Z** going? _____

   b. How fast is car **L** going? _____

   c. Which car is going faster? _____

L
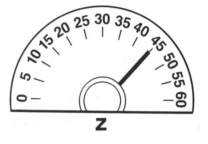
Z

13. Look at the lines in the box below.

   a. Write **1** next to each line that is 1 centimeter long.

   b. Write **2** next to each line that is 2 centimeters long.

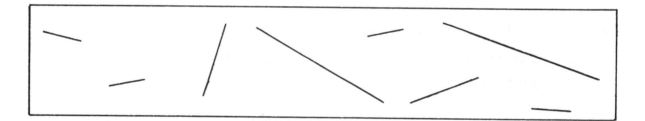

14. Look at the pictures.

   A  B

   a. One picture shows Herman when the cab is standing still.

   Which picture is that? _____

   b. One picture shows Herman when the cab is going 50 miles per hour. Which picture is that? _____

15. How many centimeters are in one meter? _____

LESSON 49

A

In today's lesson you read about temperature. Use what you learned to do these items.

1. **Fill in the blank.** When we talk about how hot or cold something

   is, we tell about the _____ of the thing.

2. **Finish the rule.** When an object gets hotter, the temperature goes

   _____.

3. When the earth gets cold, which way does the temperature go? _____

4. An oven gets hotter. So what do you know about the temperature of

   the oven? _____

Story items

5. Look at the picture below. Goad is filled up with air.

   a. Make a **dotted arrow** from her mouth to show which way the air will leave Goad.

   b. Make a **solid arrow** on Goad to show which way she will move.

6. Here's a picture of a jet.

   a. Draw a **dotted arrow** from a jet engine to show which way the air moves.

   b. Draw a **solid arrow** on the plane to show which way it will move.

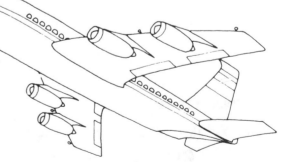

7. Pretend you are in an airplane that is flying over a city. What would

   look different about the city? _____

8. Here's how fast different things can go: **20 miles per hour**

35 miles per hour

2 hundred miles per hour

5 hundred miles per hour

  a. Which speed tells how fast a racing car can go?

_____

  b. Which speed tells how fast a jet can fly?

_____

  c. Which speed tells how fast a fast man can run?

_____

9. The plane went up and up after it left New York City. How high did

it go? _____

10. How fast did the plane fly? _____

11. When a plane goes 5 hundred miles per hour, do the passengers feel

like they're moving fast? _____

12. How many flies were on the plane? _____

Skill items

13. Compare object A and object B. Remember what you're going to tell
first and what you're going to tell next.

_____

_____

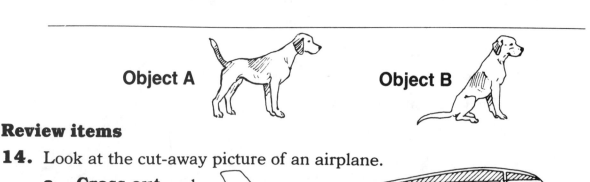

Object A   **Object B**

Review items

14. Look at the cut-away picture of an airplane.

  a. **Cross out** each
flight attendant.

  b. **Circle** the pilot.

15. Look at the map.

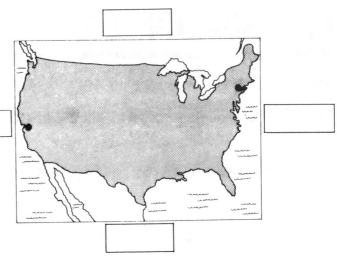

   a. Write **north, south, east,** and **west** in the right boxes.

   b. Write **L** where New York City is.

   c. Write **X** where San Francisco is.

16. How many centimeters are in one meter? _____

17. Look at the picture below.

   a. The food that three of the animals eat each day weighs as much as those animals. **Circle** those animals.

   b. The food that four of the animals eat each day does not weigh as much as those animals. **Underline** those animals.

18. a. Does a spider weigh **more than a gram** or **less than a gram?**

_____

   b. Does a toad weigh **more than a gram** or **less than a gram?**

_____

19. Look at the scale in the picture.

   a. How many grams are on the left side of the scale? _____

   b. How many ants are on the other side? _____

   c. So how much weight is on the side of the scale with the ants?

_____

LESSON 50

A

In today's lesson, you read about degrees. Use what you learned to do these items.

1. **Finish the rule.** When an object gets hotter, the temperature goes

_____.

2. **Fill in the blank.** When the temperature goes up, the number of

_____ goes up.

3. Look at the picture. It tells how many degrees each object is.

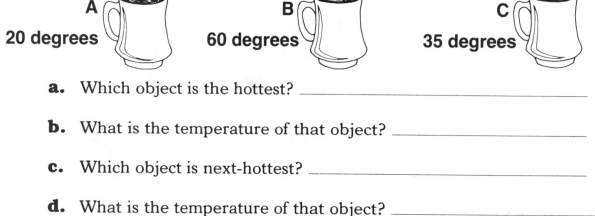

A **20 degrees**   B **60 degrees**   C **35 degrees**

   a. Which object is the hottest? _____

   b. What is the temperature of that object? _____

   c. Which object is next-hottest? _____

   d. What is the temperature of that object? _____

   e. Which object is coldest? _____

   f. What is the temperature of that object? _____

B

Review items

4. **a.** Does a water strider weigh **more than a gram** or **less than a gram?** _____

   b. Does a mole weigh **more than a gram** or **less than a gram?**

_____

5. **Finish the sentence.** When we weigh very small things, we use

_____.

6. Look at the scale in the picture.

    a. How many grams are on the left side of the scale? _____

    b. How many fleas are on the other side? _____

    c. So how much weight is on the side of the scale with the fleas?

_____

7. Circle the water striders.

8. Finish the rule. If tiny animals fall from high places, _____

_____ .

9. If a grain of sugar were very big, it would look like a piece of glass.

    a. What kind of corners does a grain of sugar have? _____

    b. Finish the sentence. A grain of sugar is no bigger than _____

_____ .

10. a. You can see drops of water on grass early in the morning. What

       are those drops called? _____

    b. Does dew form in the middle of the day? _____

    c. Circle the answer. Dew forms when the air gets _____

        • cooler   • warmer

11. Look at the picture. The dotted line shows how much water will go into the tube. **Draw the skin** that covers the top of that water.

12. These animals fell from a cliff. **Underline** the words that tell what happened to each animal.

a. pointer
wasn't hurt
was hurt
was killed

b. mouse
wasn't hurt
was hurt
was killed

c. fly
wasn't hurt
was hurt
was killed

13. a. Finish the sentence. The temperature of an object tells how

_____ that object is.

b. Finish the rule. When an object gets hotter, the temperature

goes _____.

c. When a door gets colder, which way does the temperature go?

_____

d. A jar gets hotter. So what do you know about the temperature of

the jar? _____

14. When a boy jumps this way ↖, there is a push against the ground.

Draw an arrow to show the direction of that push. _____

15. If a girl dove into a pool in this direction ↗, there would be a push against the side of the pool. Draw an arrow to show the direction of

that push. _____

16. What did people use to think would happen if your toe touched a

toad? _____

17. a. Finish the sentence. The world is called _____.

b. What is most of the world covered with? _____

18. a. Finish the sentence. The land parts of the world are divided

into _____.

b. What country do you live in? _____

19. a. Underline the ruler that will make the highest sound.

   b. Make a box around the ruler that will make the lowest sound.

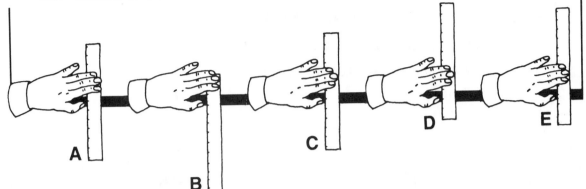

20. Some hairs in the picture are being pushed down. Some are being pulled up. Look at the skin next to each hair.

   a. Write **up** on every hair that is moving up.

   b. Write **down** on every hair that is moving down.

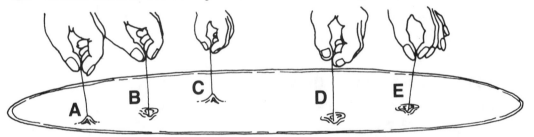

21. Look at the picture. The man is holding a stick that is one meter long.

   a. Write the letter of each object that is one meter long. _____

   b. Write the letter of each object that is two meters long. _____

22. Everybody in the picture below should be on a diet. Write what kind of diet each person should be on.

- Write **L** for a diet **to lose weight.**
- Write **P** for a diet **to put on weight.**
- Write **H** for a diet **to stay healthy.**

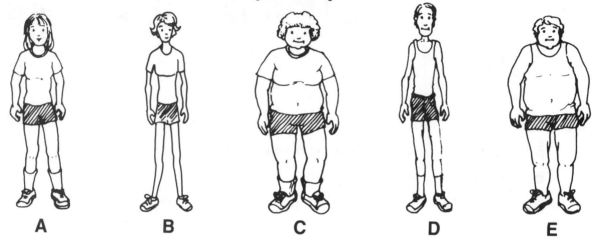

A   B   C   D   E

23. Cross out the toads in the picture.

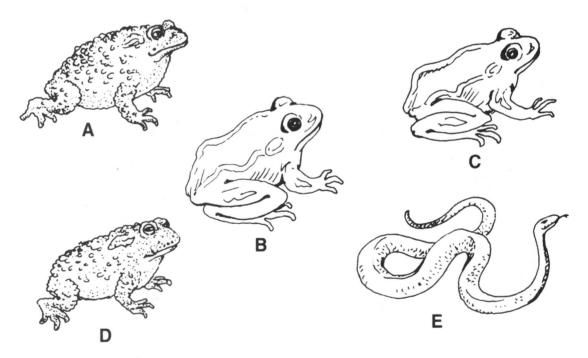

LESSON 51

A

Story items

1. **a.** Name the city on the east coast that Herman flew from.

_____

   b. Name the city on the west coast that Herman flew to.

_____

   c. How far is that trip? _____

2. **Finish the sentence.** The kitchen on an airplane is called a _____.

3. Herman went from New York City to San Francisco. Name three

   cities he flew over. ①_____

  ②_____ ③_____

4. **Circle** the pictures that show what Herman had for his meal service.

candy

salad

C

A   B

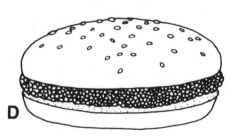

D

E

F

5. **a.** Herman took a nap on something. What was that thing?

_____

   b. Why did Herman like that place? _____

6. Look at the map below.
  a. Write **east** next to the city on the east coast.
  b. Write **west** next to the city on the west coast.
  c. **Draw an arrow** that shows the trip the jet plane took.
  d. Make a **D** where Denver is.
  e. Make a **C** where Chicago is.

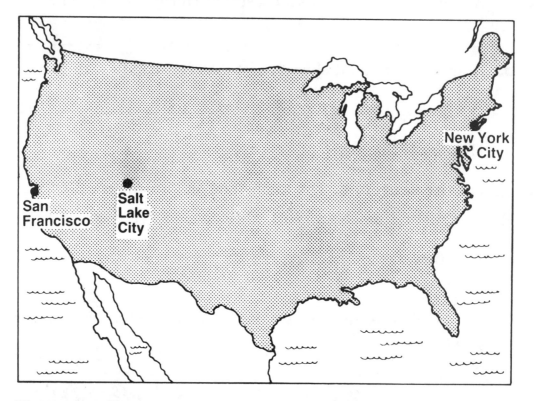

7. How many flies were on the plane when it left New York City? _____

8. How many flies got off the plane in San Francisco? _____

Skill items

9. Here's a rule: **All the crew members got off the plane.**
  a. Mr. Jones is a crew member. So what else do you know about

  Mr. Jones? _____

  b. The flight attendant is a crew member. So what else do you

  know about the flight attendant? _____

  c. Mr. Sanchez is a passenger. So what else do you know about Mr.

  Sanchez? _____

Review items

10. a. **Fill in the blank.** If you know the temperature of an object,

  you know how _____ that object is.

b. When rain gets cold, which way does the temperature go?

_____

c. A pan gets hotter. So what do you know about the temperature

of the pan? _____

11. Here's how fast different things can go: **20 miles per hour**
                                                 35 miles per hour
                                        2 hundred miles per hour
                                        5 hundred miles per hour

a. Which speed tells how fast a fast man can run?

_____

b. Which speed tells how fast a pointer can run?

_____

c. Which speed tells how fast a jet can fly?

_____

12. Fill in the blank. When the temperature goes up, the number of

_____ goes up.

13. Look at the picture of the jet.
   a. Draw a dotted arrow from an engine to show which way the air
   rushes out of the jet engine.
   b. Draw a solid arrow on the plane to show which way it will move.

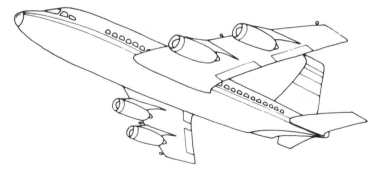

14. If a grain of sugar were very big, it would look like a piece of glass.

a. What kind of corners does a grain of sugar have? _____

b. Finish the sentence. A grain of sugar is no bigger than _____

_____.

15. a. Finish the sentence. The world is called _____.

b. What is most of the world covered with? _____

16. Finish the sentence. When we weigh very small things, we use

_____.

17. a. Finish the sentence. The land parts of the world are divided

into _____.

b. What country do you live in? _____

18. Look at the map below. Do not use your textbook.
   a. Write **north, south, east,** and **west** in the right boxes.
   b. Make a **B** where the United States is.
   c. Make a **K** where Canada is.
   d. Make a **T** where Mexico is.
   e. Make an **X** where South America is.

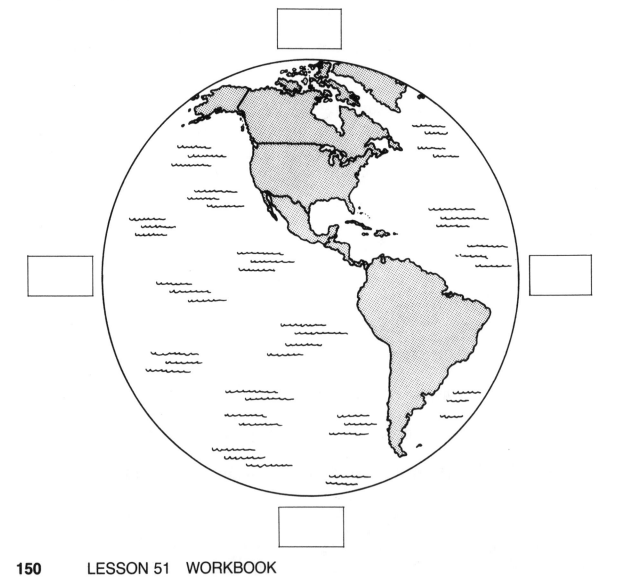

LESSON 52

A

In today's lesson, you read about finding the direction of a wind. Use what you learned to do these items.

1. Look at the picture.
   a. Write **north, south, east,** and **west** in the right boxes.
   b. Which animal is facing into the wind? _____
   c. Which direction is that animal facing? _____
   d. So what's the name of the wind? _____

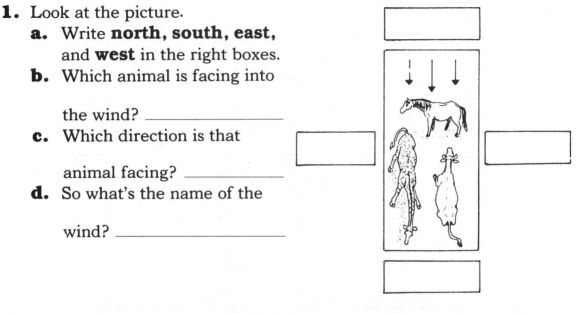

B

Story items

2. a. How many flies were on the plane when it left New York City?

   _____

   b. How many flies got off the plane in San Francisco? _____

   c. How many flies died on the plane? _____

   d. What killed them? _____

   e. What saved Herman's life? _____

3. Where did Herman stay when fly spray filled the air? _____

   _____

4. Some workers stacked some dinners in the galley. Why didn't those dinners smell very good to Herman? _____

5. Look at the map below. The Y shows where the wind starts.
   a. Write **north, south, east,** and **west** in the right boxes.
   b. Make a **Z** where San Francisco is.
   c. If you were in San Francisco, which direction would you face if

   you wanted the wind to blow in your face? _____

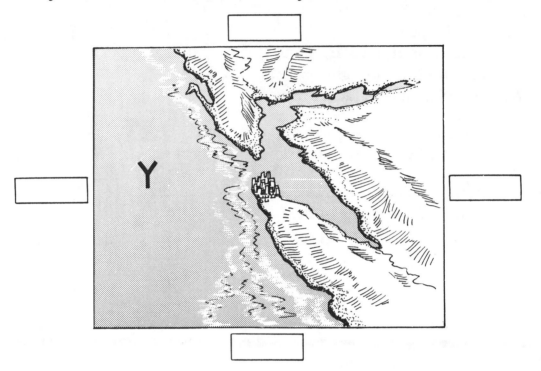

6. a. How many hours did it take to fly from New York City to

   San Francisco? _____
   b. Will it take **more time** or **less time** to fly from San Francisco

   to New York City? _____

Review items
7. Fill in the blank. When the temperature goes up, the number of

   _____ goes up.

8. a. Name three cities you might fly over if you flew from New York
   City to San Francisco.

   ① _____

   ② _____

   ③ _____

   b. How far is it from New York City to San Francisco? _____

9. Look at the picture.

   a. What is the temperature of object A? _____

   b. What is the temperature of object B? _____

   c. What is the temperature of object C? _____

   d. Which object is the hottest? _____

   e. Which object is the coldest? _____

A	B	C
10 degrees	**80 degrees**	**50 degrees**

10. Look at the lines in the box below.

   a. Write **2** next to each line that is 2 centimeters long.

   b. Write **3** next to each line that is 3 centimeters long.

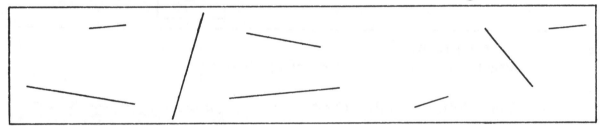

11. Look at the map below.

   a. Write **east** next to the city on the east coast.

   b. Write **west** next to the city on the west coast.

   c. **Draw an arrow** that shows the trip from New York City to San Francisco.

   d. Make a **C** where Chicago is.

   e. Make an **L** where Salt Lake City is.

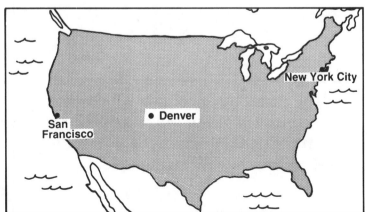

12. Here's what you see through the circles made by your hands.

9

Draw what you would see through strong binoculars.

13. Look at the map.
  a. Write **north, south, east,** and **west** in the right boxes.
  b. Make a **G** where the United States is.
  c. Make a **K** where Canada is.
  d. Make an **R** where Mexico is.
  e. Make an **A** where South America is.

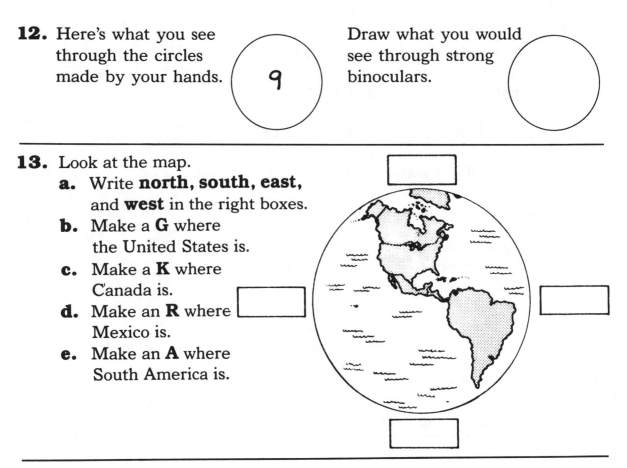

14. Look at the picture.
  a. Which letter is on the shore of the lake? _____

  b. Which letter is in the forest? _____

  c. Which letter is in the middle of the lake? _____

  d. Which letter is on the path? _____

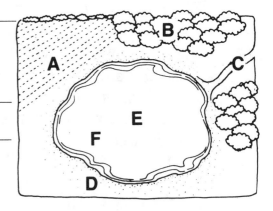

15. The dotted arrow shows which way the girl will jump. Make a **solid arrow** on the back of the boat to show which way it will move.

LESSON 53

A

In today's lesson, you read about airplanes and wind. Use what you learned to do these items.

1. a. Draw a circle around every plane that will go the fastest.

   b. Draw an arrow on the cloud in each picture to show which way it is moving.

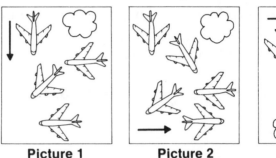 

      Picture 1   Picture 2   Picture 3

B

Story items

2. What month was it when Herman landed in San Francisco? _____

3. a. What was the temperature when Herman landed in San Francisco? _____

   b. Was it **hotter** or **colder** in San Francisco when the plane left there? _____

4. Look at the map.

   a. Write **north, south, east,** and **west** in the right boxes.

   b. Draw an arrow on the cloud to show which way the cloud will move.

   c. Fill in the blanks. That wind is blowing from the _____. So that wind is called

_____ .

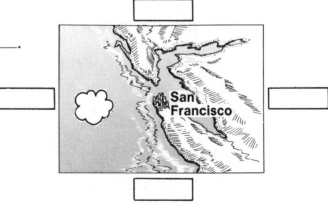

5. What made the trip to New York City a rough trip? _____

6. Why did the captain tell the passengers to keep their seat belts

fastened? _____

7. a. Did the passengers enjoy the trip? _____

    b. Tell why. _____

8. a. How long did the trip to San Francisco take? _____

    b. How long did the trip back to New York City take? _____

    c. Tell why the trip back to New York City took less time. _____

Skill items

9. Compare object A and object B. Remember what you're going to tell first and what you're going to tell next.

_____

_____

_____

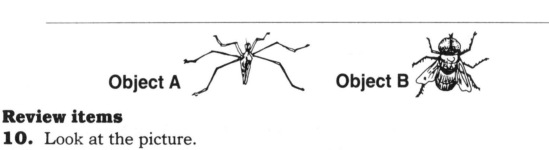

Object A   **Object B**

Review items

10. Look at the picture.

    a. Write **north, south, east,** and **west** in the right boxes.

    b. Which animal is facing into the wind? _____

    c. Which direction is that animal facing? _____

    d. So what's the name of the wind? _____

11. Look at the picture.
   a. Write **north**, **south**, **east**, and **west** in the right boxes.
   b. Make an **M** where Mexico is.
   c. Make a **C** where Canada is.
   d. Make an **F** where South America is.
   e. Make a **U** where the United States is.

12. a. How many legs does an insect have? _____

   b. How many legs does a fly have? _____

   c. How many legs does a flea have? _____

   d. How many legs does an ant have? _____

   e. How many legs does a horse have? _____

   f. How many legs does a spider have? _____

13. Look at the map below. The **Y** shows where the wind starts.
   a. Write **north, south, east,** and **west** in the right boxes.
   b. Make an **R** where San Francisco is.
   c. If you were in San Francisco, which direction would you face if you wanted the wind to blow

   in your face? _____

14. Some things in the picture below weigh 1 gram. Some weigh 2 grams. Some weigh 5 grams. Fill in the blanks to tell how much each object weighs.

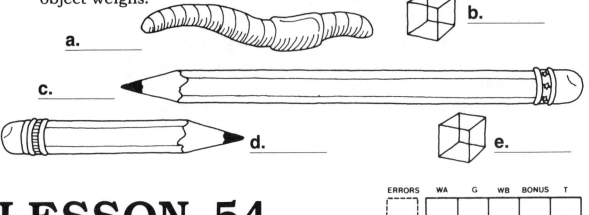

a. _____

b. _____

c. _____

d. _____

e. _____

LESSON 54

ERRORS	WA	G	WB	BONUS	T

A

In today's lesson, you read more about the world. Use what you learned to do these items.

1. Look at the map .
    a. Write **north, south, east,** and **west** in the right boxes.
    b. Make an **H** where New York City is.
    c. Make an **I** where San Francisco is.
    d. Make a **J** where Japan is.
    e. Make a **P** where the Pacific Ocean is.

B

Story items

2. a. Did the fly spray kill Herman? _____

    b. Tell why. _____

3. a. After the plane left New York City, where did it stop first?

_____

b. Finish the sentence. Then the plane left for _____.

c. In what direction did the plane fly? _____

4. How far is it from New York City to San Francisco?

_____

5. How far is it from San Francisco to Japan?

_____

6. What ocean do you cross to get from San Francisco to Japan?

_____

7. What did Herman get stuck in? _____

8. Cross out Herman's enemy.

A   B   C

Skill items

9. Here's a rule: **Every worker cleaned the plane.**

    a. Joe was a worker. So what else do you know about Joe?

_____

    b. Helen was a worker. So what else do you know about Helen?

_____

    c. Stella was a worker. So what else do you know about Stella?

_____

Review items

10. a. In each picture below, **draw a circle** around every plane that
will go the fastest.

    b. Draw an arrow on the cloud in each picture to show which way
it is moving.

Picture A 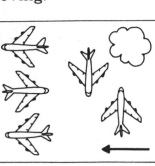   **Picture B**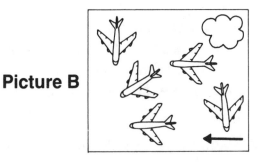

11. Here's how fast different things can go:

20 miles per hour	2 hundred miles per hour
35 miles per hour	5 hundred miles per hour

    a. Which speed tells how fast a jet can fly?

_____

    b. Which speed tells how fast a pointer can run?

_____

12. Look at the map.
    a. Write **north, south, east,** and **west** in the right boxes.
    b. **Draw an arrow** on the cloud to show which way the cloud will move.
    c. What's the name of the wind that will move

the cloud? _____

13. Finish the rule. When something moves in one direction, _____

_____.

14. **a.** Which grow up faster, mice or dogs? _____

    b. Which grow up faster, boys or girls? _____

15. **a.** **Finish the sentence.** If an ant weighed as much as a beagle,

the ant could carry an object as heavy as _____.

    b. How many ants would it take to weigh as much as a peanut? _____

16. Look at the picture.
    a. Write **north, south, east,** and **west** in the right boxes.
    b. An arrow goes from the B. Which direction is that

arrow going? _____
    c. **Make an arrow** that goes west from the T.
    d. **Draw the smoke** in the picture.

17. What do a mole's legs look like? _____

LESSON 55

A In today's lesson, you read about the eye of a fly. Use what you learned to do these items.

1. a. Which eye works like one drop, a human's eye or a fly's eye?

_____

b. Which eye works like many drops? _____

B

Story items
Fill in the blanks for the items.

2. a. The United States is not a state. It is a _____.

b. Japan is a _____.

3. The United States is made up of fifty _____.

4. The biggest state in the United States is _____.

5. The second-biggest state in the United States is _____.

6. The third-biggest state in the United States is _____.

7. The whole country of Japan is not as big as the state of _____.

Review items

8. Here's how fast different things can go: **20 miles per hour**
35 miles per hour
2 hundred miles per hour
5 hundred miles per hour

a. Which speed tells how fast a fast man can run?

_____

b. Which speed tells how fast a jet can fly?

_____

c. Which speed tells how fast a pointer can run?

_____

9. a. Finish the sentence. If an ant weighed as much as an elephant, the ant could carry an object as heavy as _____.

b. How many ants would it take to weigh as much as a peanut? ____

10. a. Make a box around the ruler that will make the highest sound.

b. Underline the ruler that will make the lowest sound.

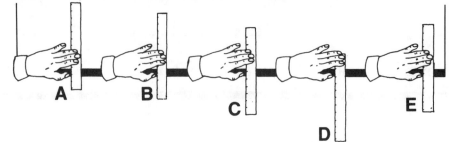

11. If a grain of sugar were very big, it would look like a piece of glass.

a. What kind of corners does a grain of sugar have? _____

b. Finish the sentence. A grain of sugar is no bigger than _____

_____.

12. a. You can see drops of water on grass early in the morning. What are those drops called? _____

b. Does dew form in the middle of the day? _____

c. Underline the answer. Dew forms when the air gets _____

• warmer   • cooler

13. Some hairs in the picture are being pushed down. Some are being pulled up. Look at the skin next to each hair.

a. Write **up** on every hair that is moving up.

b. Write **down** on every hair that is moving down.

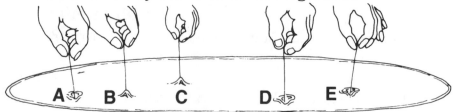

14. Circle the water striders.

15. Look at the map below.
 a. Write **north, south, east,** and **west** in the right boxes.
 b. Write **X** where New York City is.
 c. Write **Y** where San Francisco is.
 d. Write **P** where Japan is.
 e. Write **T** where
   the Pacific Ocean is.

16. Some things happen as tadpoles grow.
 a. **Underline** what happens first.
 b. **Cross out** what happens last.
   • They grow back legs.
   • They grow front legs.
   • Their tails disappear.

17. a. In which direction do you fly to get from San Francisco to

   Japan? _____

 b. How far is it from San Francisco to Japan? _____

 c. What ocean do you cross between San Francisco and Japan?

   _____

18. Some people in the picture are holding sticks that are 1 meter long.
   Write **1 meter** under each stick that is 1 meter long.

A   B   C   D   E

19. Underline the animals that live on the land.

20. a. Does a horse weigh **more than a gram** or **less than a gram?**

_____

b. Does a spider weigh **more than a gram** or **less than a gram?**

_____

21. Here's what you see through strong binoculars.

Draw what you would see through the circles made by your hands.

22. Draw an arrow at A and an arrow at B to show which way the string will move when the toad moves the blue fly.

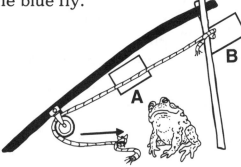

23. Look at the picture below.
   a. Make an arrow **over** each canoe to show which way the canoe is moving.
   b. Make an arrow **under** each paddle to show which way the paddle is moving in the water.

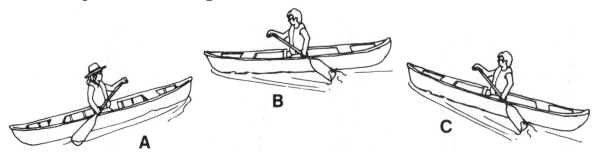

LESSON 56

A

In today's lesson, you read about spiders. Use what you learned to do these items.

1. a. Some of the objects in the picture are insects, and some are spiders. **Circle** the spiders.

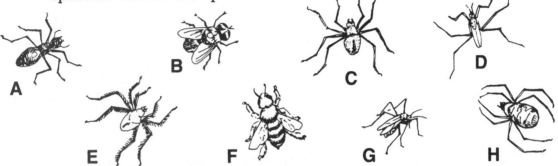

A B C D E F G H

    b. Object D is not a spider. Tell why. _____

_____

2. a. How many legs does an insect have? _____ _____

    b. How many legs does a fly have? _____

    c. How many legs does a flea have? _____

    d. How many legs does a spider have? _____

    e. How many legs does a water strider have? _____

    f. How many legs does an ant have? _____

B

Story items

3. Why did Herman have a hard time escaping from the spider web?

_____

4. How do most spiders kill insects? _____

5. Did the spider kill Herman? _____

6. Finish the sentence. When a spider wraps an insect in a web, the insect looks like a _____ .

7. Look at the picture.
   a. Circle the spider.
   b. Cross out Herman.
   c. Make a box around the dead insect.

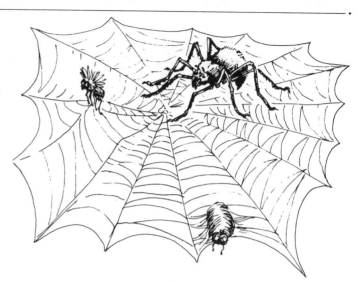

8. Herman took a nap on something that was warm and red. What was

it? _____

9. a. What country was the plane flying to? _____

   b. In which direction did the plane fly? _____
   c. How far is it from San Francisco to that country?

   _____

   d. What ocean did the plane cross? _____
10. Look at the picture.
   a. What country is shown in the picture? _____
   b. Make an **X** on the mountain.

Review items

11. Look at the map below.
  a. Write **east** next to the city on the east coast.
  b. Write **west** next to the city on the west coast.
  c. Make a **C** where Chicago is.
  d. Make a **D** where Denver is.

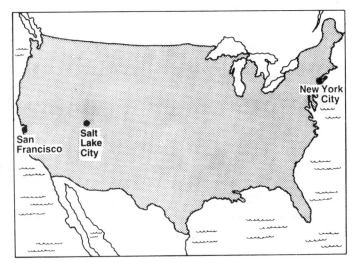

12. Finish each sentence.
  a. The United States is not a city. It is a _____.

  b. Japan is not a state. It is a _____.

  c. The United States is made up of fifty _____.

13. Finish each sentence.
  a. The biggest state in the United States is _____.

  b. The second-biggest state in the United States is _____.

  c. The third-biggest state in the United States is _____.

14. Look at the pictures below.

  a. One picture shows Herman when the cab is going 35 miles per

   hour. Which picture is that? _____

  b. One picture shows Herman when the cab is standing still. Which

   picture is that? _____

15. Fill in the blank. The _____ inside a car tells how fast the car is moving.

16. Each speedometer in the picture shows how fast the car is moving.

   a. How fast is car **J** going? _____

   b. How fast is car **K** going? _____

   c. Which car is going faster? _____

J

K

17. a. Cross out the youngest fly.
     b. Circle the oldest fly.

A   B   C   D

18. a. Finish the sentence. When flies are born, they are worms

   called _____.

   b. Do flies change size **on the inside** or **on the outside?** _____

   _____

19. a. Which eye works like many drops, a human's eye or a fly's eye?

   _____

   b. Which eye works like one drop? _____

LESSON 57

A

Story items

1. Name a state in the United States that is bigger than Japan. _____

2. a. Let's say that you are outside when the temperature is 10

degrees. What is the temperature inside your body? _____

   b. Let's say you are outside when it is 45 degrees. What is the

temperature inside your body? _____

3. a. Let's say a fly is outside when the temperature is 10 degrees.

What is the temperature inside the fly's body? _____

   b. Let's say a fly is outside when the temperature is 45 degrees.

What is the temperature inside the fly's body? _____

4. a. Would it be easier to catch a fly **on a hot day** or **on a cold**

day? _____

   b. Tell why. _____

5. Why did Herman want to get out of the jet? _____

_____

6. Write **warm-blooded** after each animal that is warm-blooded.

   a. Herman _____

   b. fly _____

   c. ant _____

   d. dog _____

   e. cat _____

   f. flea _____

   g. water strider _____

   h. horse _____

Skill items

7. Compare object A and object B. Remember what you're going to tell first and what you're going to tell next.

_____

_____

_____

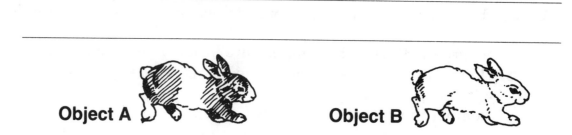

Object A   **Object B**

Review items

8. a. Some of the things in the picture below are insects and some are spiders. **Underline** the spiders.

b. Object C is not a spider. Tell why.

_____

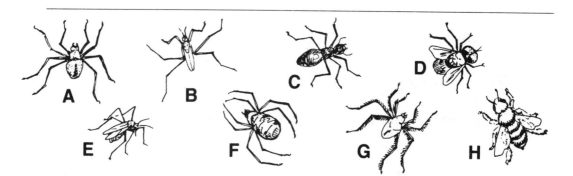

9. Look at the picture below. Each speedometer in the picture shows how fast the truck is moving.

a. How fast is truck **A** going? _____

b. How fast is truck **B** going? _____

c. Which truck is going faster? _____

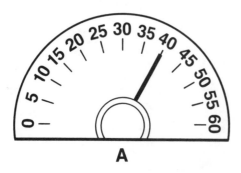

A

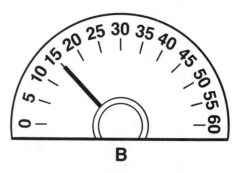

B

10. a. How many legs does a fly have? _____

b. How many legs does an ant have? _____

c. How many legs does a spider have? _____

d. How many legs does a flea have? _____

e. How many legs does an insect have? _____

f. How many legs does a water strider have? _____

11. a. How do most spiders kill insects? _____

b. Finish the sentence. When a spider wraps an insect in a web,

the insect looks like a _____

12. Look at the map below.

a. Write **north, south, east,** and **west** in the right boxes.

b. Make an **F** where San Francisco is.

c. Make a **C** where Chicago is.

d. Make an **X** where New York City is.

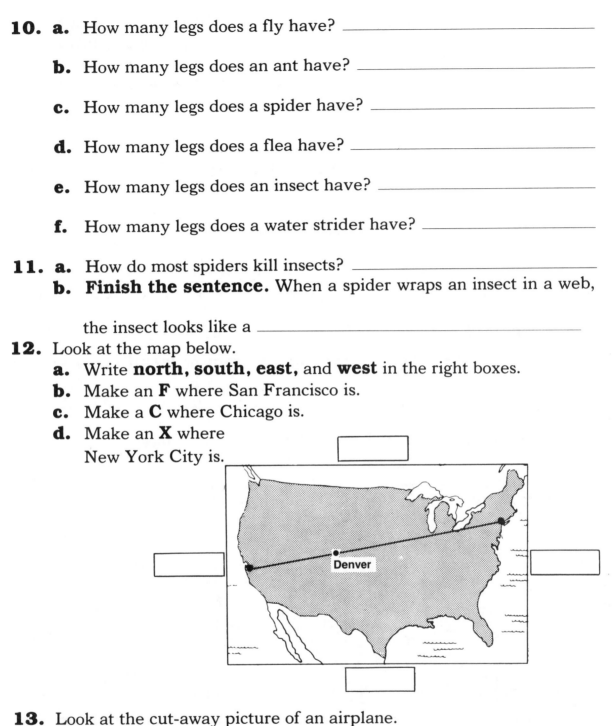

13. Look at the cut-away picture of an airplane.

a. Circle each flight attendant.

b. Cross out the pilot.

14. Here's how fast different things can go: **20 miles per hour**
                                                  35 miles per hour
                                      2 hundred miles per hour
                                      5 hundred miles per hour

a. Which speed tells how fast a jet can fly?

_____

b. Which speed tells how fast a fast man can run?

_____

c. Which speed tells how fast a pointer can run?

_____

15. a. Does an apple weigh **more than a gram** or **less than a**

gram? _____

b. Does a flea weigh **more than a gram** or **less than a gram?**

_____

16. Finish the rule. If tiny animals fall from high places, _____.

17. Cross out the animals that live on the land.

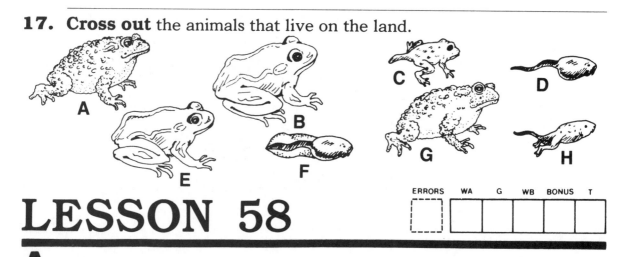

LESSON 58

ERRORS	WA	G	WB	BONUS	T

A In today's lesson, you read about the air around the earth. Use what you learned to do these items.

1. Jean is 2 miles high. Fran is 5 miles high.

a. Who is colder? _____

b. Tell why. _____

_____

2. Circle the plane in the picture that is in the coldest air.

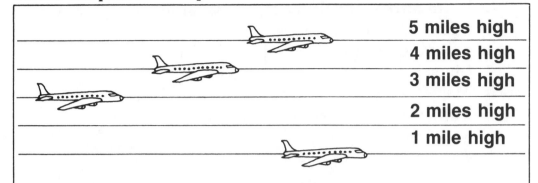

	5 miles high
	4 miles high
	3 miles high
	2 miles high
	1 mile high

Story items

3. a. Why was Herman moving so slowly at the beginning of the story? _____

  b. What made Herman start moving faster? _____

4. a. After the plane took off. how high did it go? _____

  b. What was the temperature inside the plane? _____

  c. What was the temperature outside the plane? _____

5. a. What country did the plane leave? _____

  b. Where was the plane going? _____

  c. How far is that trip? _____

  d. How long should that trip take? _____

  e. Name two countries the plane flew over on the trip.

  ① _____ ② _____

6. Name a state in the United States that is bigger than Italy.

_____

7. Finish the sentence. Italy is shaped something like a _____.

8. When could Herman move fastest? **Underline the answer.**

- When it is 30 degrees.   • When it is 20 degrees.

- When it is 40 degrees.   • When it is 10 degrees.

9. Look at the map below.
   a. Write **north, south, east,** and **west** in the right boxes.
   b. Make a **J** where Japan is.
   c. Make a **C** where China is.
   d. Make a **T** where Turkey is.
   e. Make an **I** where Italy is.

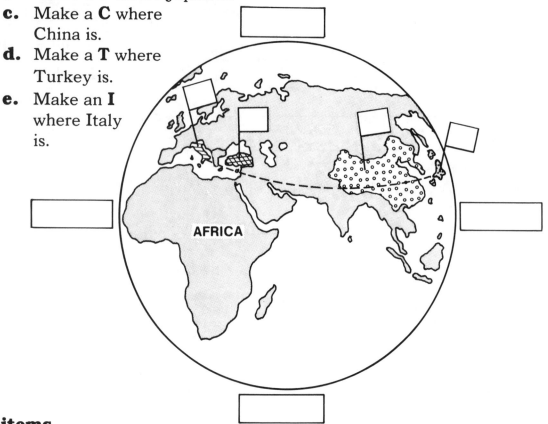

AFRICA

Skill items

10. Here's a rule: **Every insect moved slowly.**
   a. Herman was an insect. So what else do you know about

      Herman? _____

   b. A spider is not an insect. So what else do you know about a

      spider? _____

   c. A turtle is not an insect. So what else do you know about a

      turtle? _____

Review items

11. a. Which state in the United States is the biggest state? _____

   b. The second-biggest state in the United States is _____.

   c. The third-biggest state in the United States is _____.

   d. Name a state in the United States that is bigger than Japan.

   _____

12. Look at the picture of the balloon.

    a. Make a dotted arrow to show which way the air will leave the balloon.

    b. Make a solid arrow on the balloon to show which way it will move.

13. Write **warm-blooded** after each animal that is warm-blooded.

    a. spider _____

    b. boy _____

    c. cow _____

    d. flea _____

    e. horse _____

    f. fly _____

    g. beagle _____

14. a. Let's say you are outside when the temperature is 30 degrees.

    What is the temperature inside your body? _____

    b. Let's say a fly is outside when the temperature is 30 degrees.

    What is the temperature inside the fly's body? _____

15. Look at the picture. It tells how many degrees each object is.

    a. Which object is the hottest? _____

    b. What is the temperature of that object? _____

    c. Which object is the coldest? _____

    d. What is the temperature of that object? _____

A   50 degrees

B   60 degrees

C   40 degrees

16. Look at the scale in the picture.
   a. How many grams are on the left side of the scale? _____

   b. How many beetles are on the other side? _____
   c. So how much weight is on the side of the scale with the beetles?

_____

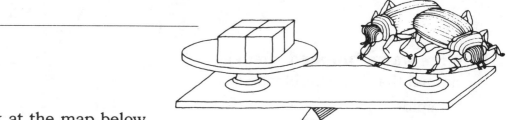

17. Look at the map below.
   • Things that are this far apart on the map ⟷ are 2 miles apart.
   • Things that are this far apart ⟷ are 4 miles apart.
   a. Write **2** in the circle if the line stands for 2 miles.
   b. Write **4** in the circle if the line stands for 4 miles.
   c. How far is it from the police station to the swimming pool?

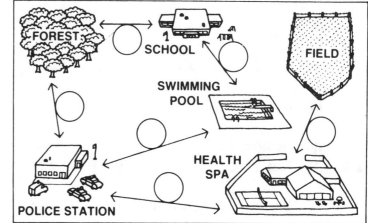

LESSON 59

ERRORS	WA	G	WB	BONUS	T

A

Story items
   1. Name something that would smell good to Herman.

_____

   2. Name something that would smell bad to Herman.

_____

   3. a. After the plane left Italy, what direction did it fly? _____

b. What airport did it fly to? _____

c. What city is that airport in? _____

4. Where are the gas tanks on a big jet? _____

5. Why was it hard for Herman to move around in the fall? _____

_____

6. What killed Herman? _____

7. Look at the map.
  a. Make an **A** where Italy is.
  b. Make a **B** where New York City is.

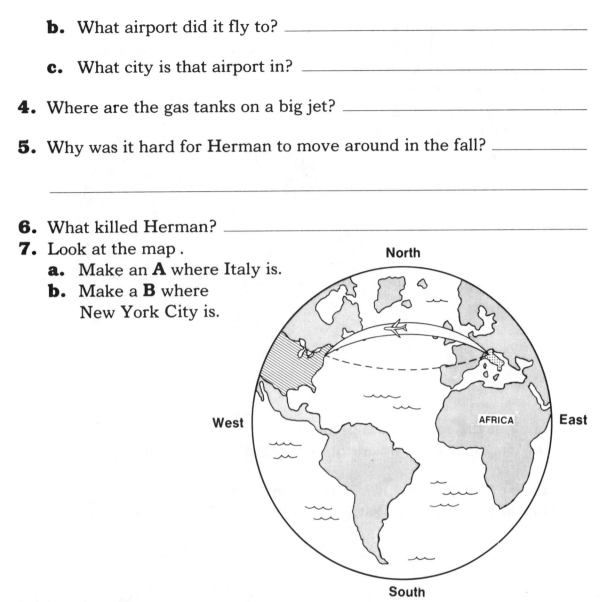

Review items

8. a. Name a state in the United States that is bigger than Italy.

_____

  b. Finish the sentence. Italy is shaped something like a _____.

9. Some lines in the box below are 1 centimeter long. Write **1 centimeter** next to each of those lines.

10. Look at the map below.

    a. Write **north, south, east,** and **west** in the right boxes.

    b. Make an **I** where Italy is.

    c. Make a **T** where Turkey is.

    d. Make a **C** where China is.

    e. Make a **J** where Japan is.

AFRICA

11. Look at the scale in the picture.

    a. How many grams are on the left side of the scale? _____

    b. How many ants are on the other side? _____

    c. So how much weight is on the side of the scale with the ants?

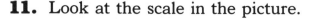

12. The dotted arrow shows which way the boy will jump. **Make a solid arrow** on the block of ice to show which way it will move.

13. Look at the map below. Do not use your textbook.
  a. Write **north, south, east,** and **west** in the right boxes.
  b. Make a **U** where the United States is.
  c. Make a **C** where Canada is.
  d. Make an **M** where Mexico is.
  e. Make an **A** where South America is.

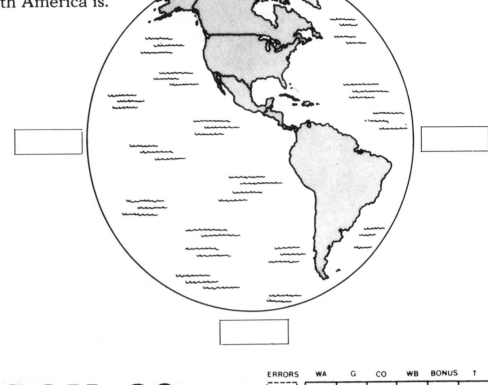

LESSON 60

ERRORS	WA	G	CO	WB	BONUS	T

A

Story items

1. The picture shows the first two rows of the word bank. Three words do not belong in this part of the word bank. **Circle** the words that do not belong.

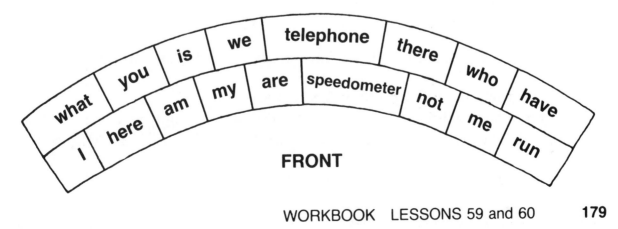

FRONT

2. The people in Hohoboho only did one thing. What was that?

_____

3. Finish the sentence. All the words in Hohoboho stayed in a

strange place called _____.

Skill items

4. Compare object A and object B. Remember what you're going to tell first and what you're going to tell next.

_____

_____

_____

Object A

Object B

Review items

5. Fill in the blanks.

A man had five fleas. When those fleas lined up end to end, they

were _____ long.

The man had a pencil. It was a short pencil. So it weighed

_____.

The man had three dogs. Two of them were the same size. They

were a poodle and a pointer. They were _____
long. The third dog the man had looked something like a pointer, but it was shorter. It was brown and white and black. That dog could

have been a _____.

The man liked to go places. He ran a lot and he was very fast. He

could run _____ .

The man liked to run with his dogs. His pointer was very fast. It

could run _____ .

The man liked to fly in airplanes. He loved jets because they can

fly at the speed of _____ .

These jets are so fast that they can fly from New York City to San

Francisco in _____ hours. The flight from New York

City to San Francisco is _____ miles.

6. Write the name of each animal in the blank.

a. _____

c. _____

b. _____

d. _____

7. Everybody in the picture will race.
  a. Write the name of each racer in the space below the racer.
  b. Put a **1** next to the racer who will win.
  c. Put a **2** next to the racer who will come in next.
  d. Put a **3** next to the racer who will come in last.

  e. How **fast** will animal B run? _____

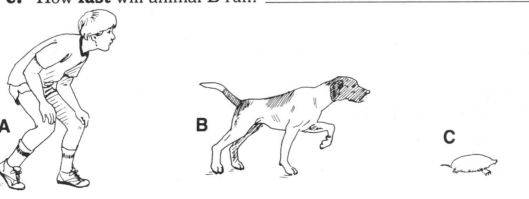

A   B   C

_____   _____   _____

8. Look at the map below.
   a. Write **north, south, east,** and **west** in the right boxes.
   b. Make a **Y** where New York City is.
   c. Make an **F** where San Francisco is.

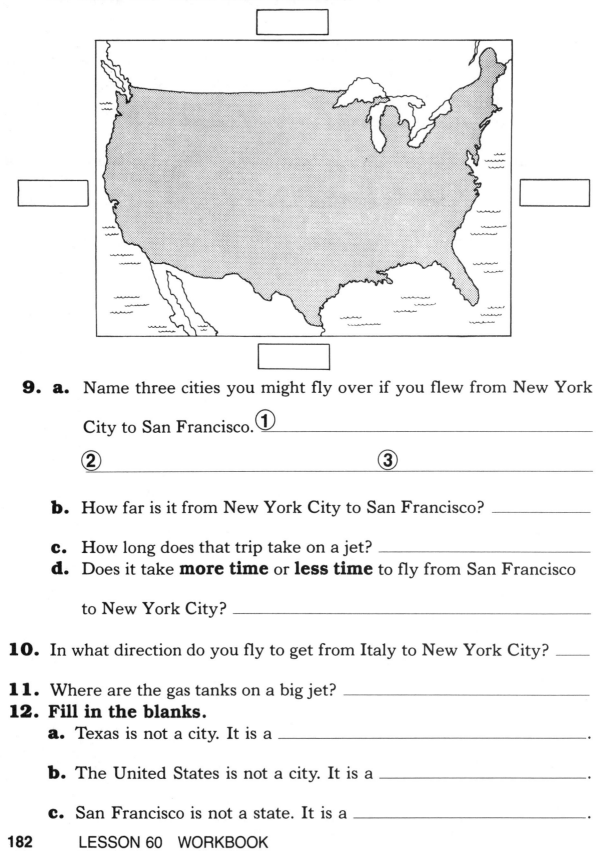

9. a. Name three cities you might fly over if you flew from New York

City to San Francisco. ① _____

   ② _____ ③ _____

   b. How far is it from New York City to San Francisco? _____

   c. How long does that trip take on a jet? _____

   d. Does it take **more time** or **less time** to fly from San Francisco

   to New York City? _____

10. In what direction do you fly to get from Italy to New York City? _____

11. Where are the gas tanks on a big jet? _____

12. Fill in the blanks.
   a. Texas is not a city. It is a _____.

   b. The United States is not a city. It is a _____.

   c. San Francisco is not a state. It is a _____.

182   LESSON 60   WORKBOOK

13. Look at the map.
   a. Write **north, south, east,** and **west** in the right boxes.
   b. Make an **0** where Italy is.
   c. Make a **J** where New York City is.

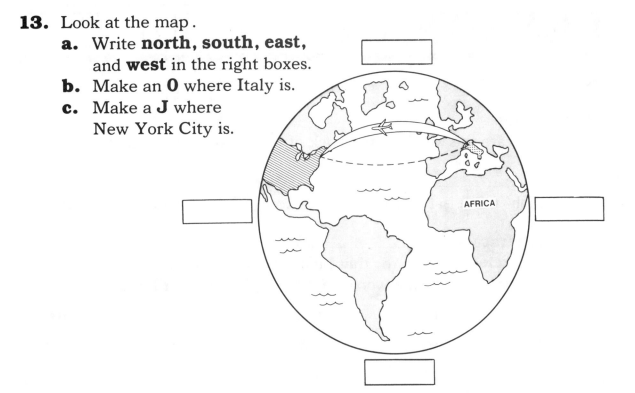

14. a. Does a pencil weigh **more than a gram** or **less than a gram?**

_____

   b. Does a frog weigh **more than a gram** or **less than a gram?**

_____

15. The dotted arrow shows which way the bullet will leave the gun. Make a solid arrow on the gun to show which way it will move.

16. a. Finish the sentence. The world is called _____ .

   b. What is most of the world covered with? _____

17. Some lines in the box below are one centimeter long. **Circle** the lines that are one centimeter long.

LESSON 61

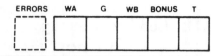

A

Story items

1. Why were the words in the back of the word bank so sad? _____

_____

2. Which word sat closer to the front of the word bank, **run** or

temperature? _____

3. a. **Circle** all the words that belong to the **sit** family.
   b. **Cross out** all the words that belong to the **run** family.

jump	hiding	runner	sat	glass
book	see	cup	rider	hot
eats	ran	sits	sitting	running
sitter	flying	runs	talked	sit

4. Name three relatives of the word **walk.**

① _____ ② _____ ③ _____

5. a. Which word sat closer to the front of the word bank, **running** or

   maggot? _____

   b. So which word was happier? _____
6. Name three relatives of the word **jump.**

① _____ ② _____ ③ _____

Skill items

7. Here's a rule: **All the words in the front row were happy.**
   a. The word **run** was not in the front row. So what else do you

   know about the word **run?** _____
   b. The word **eat** was in the back row. So what else do you know

   about the word **eat?** _____
   c. The word **temperature** was not in the front row. So what else
   do you know about the word **temperature?**

_____

Review items

8. Everybody in the picture will race.

    a. Write the name of each racer in the space below the racer.

    b. Write a **1** next to the racer who will win.

    c. Write a **2** next to the racer who will come in next.

    d. Write a **3** next to the racer who will come in last.

    e. How fast will animal C run? _____

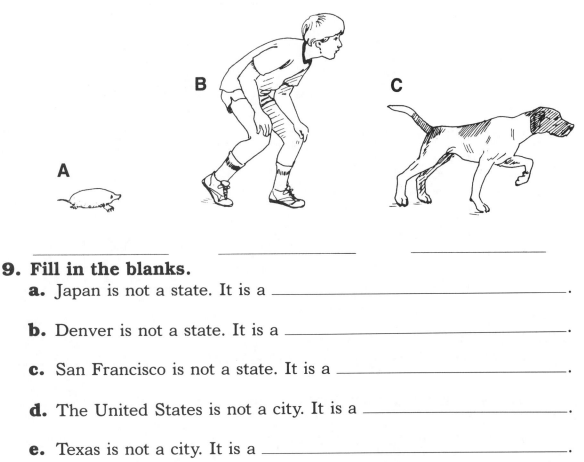

_____   _____   _____

9. Fill in the blanks.

    a. Japan is not a state. It is a _____.

    b. Denver is not a state. It is a _____.

    c. San Francisco is not a state. It is a _____.

    d. The United States is not a city. It is a _____.

    e. Texas is not a city. It is a _____.

10. Figure out how tall each animal in the picture is. You know how tall one of the animals is.

  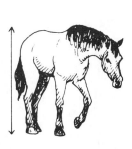

  A   **B**   **C**   **D**

11. Look at the map below.

    a. Write **north, south, east,** and **west** in the right boxes.

    b. Make a **K** where New York City is.

    c. Make an **F** where San Francisco is.

    d. Make a **P** where Chicago is.

    e. Make an **X** where Denver is.

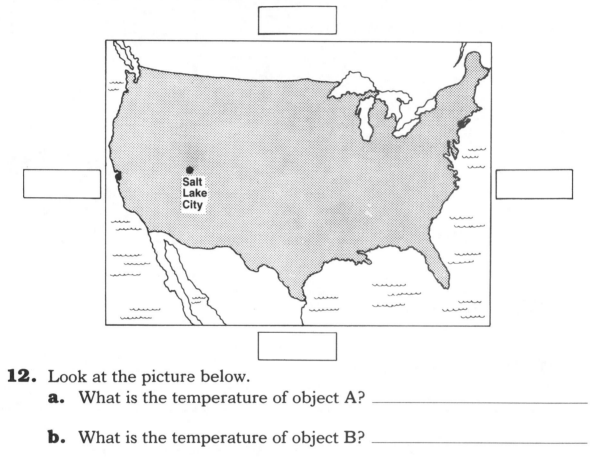

12. Look at the picture below.

    a. What is the temperature of object A? _____

    b. What is the temperature of object B? _____

    c. What is the temperature of object C? _____

    d. Which object is the hottest? _____

    e. Which object is the coldest? _____

       A   B   C

80 degrees   **50 degrees**   **70 degrees**

13. Look at the map .
  a. Write **north, south, east,** and **west** in the right boxes.
  b. Make an **I** where Italy is.
  c. Make an **M** where
      New York City is.

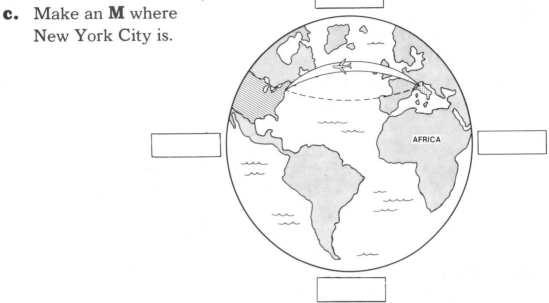

14. Look at the picture. The man is holding a stick that is one meter long.
  a. Write the letter of each object that is one meter long. _____

  b. Write the letter of each object that is two meters long. _____

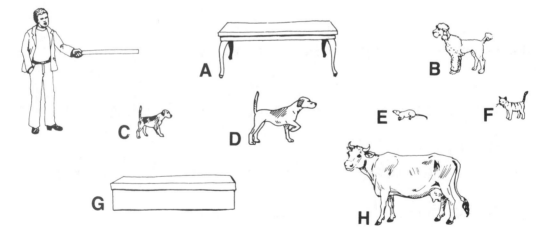

15. Some lines in the box below are **not** one centimeter long. **Cross out** the lines that are **not** one centimeter long.

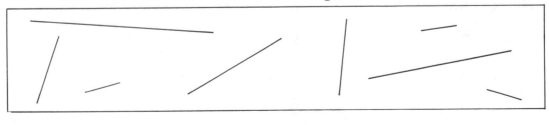

LESSON 62

A In today's lesson, you learned about ocean liners. Use what you learned to do these items.

1. Look at the picture of an ocean liner.
   a. Put a **B** on two bulkheads.
   b. Put an **X** on two decks.
   c. Put a **P** at the prow.
   d. Put an **S** at the stern.

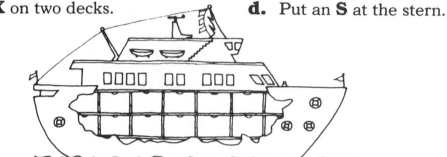

Story items

2. On what day did the words in the word bank get moved? _____

3. Let's say that the word **paper** was said more often. Would **paper** get moved **toward the front** or **toward the back** of the word bank?

   _____

4. Let's say that the word **passenger** was moved toward the back of the word bank. Was **passenger** said **more often** or **less often?**

   _____

5. When a word got moved up in the word bank, how did the word

   feel? _____

6. What was the only thing that the people in Hohoboho did before the

   big change? _____

7. Name three things that the people in Hohoboho started to do after

   the big change. ①_____

   ②_____ ③_____

Review items

8. **a.** Name three relatives of the word **jump.**

   ①_____ ②_____ ③_____

   b. Name three relatives of the word **run.**

   ①_____ ②_____ ③_____

9. Look at the picture.

   a. Write **north, south, east,** and **west** in the right boxes.

   b. Which animal is facing into the wind? _____

   c. Which direction is that animal facing? _____

   d. So what's the name of the wind? _____

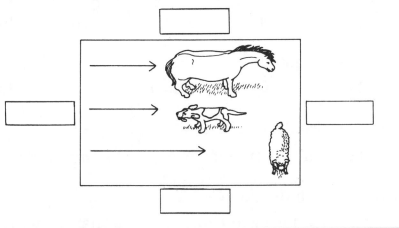

10. Look at the map below.

   a. Write **north, south, east,** and **west** in the right boxes.

   b. Make a **C** where Canada is.

   c. Make an **M** where Mexico is.

   d. Make an **X** where South America is.

   e. Make a **U** where the United States is.

11. Fill in the blanks.

Liz liked cool weather. It was the middle of summer, and she wanted to go to a city that was cool in the summer. So she went to

the city of _____.

Liz knew that the temperature of an object tells how _____ that object is. When she left New York City, the air on the ground was 30 degrees. But when the plane went higher and higher, the air

outside the plane got _____.

When the plane was 6 miles high, the air outside the plane was

below zero. It was _____.

When the plane went from New York City to San Francisco, it

was going in which direction? _____

The plane was facing the wind, so the name of the wind was a

_____.

Did the plane go **faster** or **slower** than a plane going in the

opposite direction? _____.

The air that rushed from the jet engines was going to the east, so

the jet engines moved toward the _____.
The jet engines were attached to parts of the plane. Those parts

were the _____.

As Liz flew along, she wanted to get a good look at things on the ground below. So she looked through something that makes things

look very big. She looked through _____.
She saw the city of Chicago. That city was between Denver and

_____.

12. Figure out how tall each animal in the picture is. You know how tall one of the animals is.

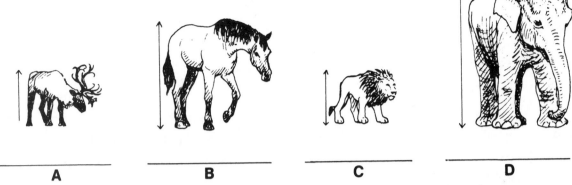

A   B   C   D

13. Underline the plane in the picture that is in the coldest air.

	5 miles high
	4 miles high
	3 miles high
	2 miles high
	1 mile high

LESSON 63

ERRORS	WA	G	WB	BONUS	T

A

In today's lesson, you read about lifeboats. Use what you learned to do these items.

1. Finish the sentence. Lifeboats are carried on _____ .

2. When are lifeboats used? _____

Story items

3. How long did the announcements in the word bank usually take?

_____

4. Did the announcements take **more time** or **less time** on the Friday

after the big change? _____

5. Name three words that got moved over 100 rows toward the front of

the word bank. ① _____ ② _____ ③ _____

6. Name two words that had to leave row 1.

①_____ ②_____

7. Let's say that the word **and** got moved from row 1 to row 30. What

do you know about how often **and** was said? _____

_____

8. Here's how often some words were said each day in Hohoboho. Some
words sit in row 8. Some words sit in row 1. **Circle** the words that sit in
row 1.

- **is** was said 120 times.
- **had** was said 110 times.
- **good** was said 3 times
- **other** was said 2 times.
- **none** was said 5 times.
- **sit** was said 105 times.

- **run** was said 100 times.
- **book** was said 4 times.
- **me** was said 109 times.
- **glass** was said 6 times.
- **he** was said 98 times.
- **climb** was said 104 times.

Skill items

9. Compare object A and object B. Remember what you're going to tell
first and what you're going to tell next.

_____

_____

_____

Object A  Object B

Review items

10. a. In which direction do you fly to get from San Francisco to

Japan? _____

b. How far is it from San Francisco to Japan? _____

_____

c. What ocean do you cross to get from San Francisco to Japan?

_____

11. Look at the columns of words below.
   a. Underline all the words in the **jump** family.
   b. Circle all the words in the **run** family.

sitting	jumper	running	jumped
runner	apple	danced	runs
jump	reading	jumping	writing
eat	ran	ruler	run

12. a. Name a state in the United States that is bigger than Italy. _____

   b. Finish the sentence. Italy is shaped something like a _____ .

13. Here is a picture of an ocean liner.
   a. Put a **K** on two bulkheads.
   b. Put an **E** on two decks.
   c. Put a **T** at the prow.
   d. Put an **R** at the stern.

14. Look at the map below. The **Y** shows where the wind starts.
   a. Write **north, south, east,** and **west** in the right boxes.
   b. Make a **Z** where San Francisco is.
   c. If you were in San Francisco, which direction would you face if

   you wanted the wind to blow in your face? _____

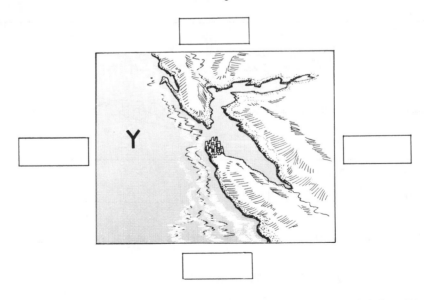

15. Look at the map below.

    a. Write **north, south, east,** and **west** in the right boxes.

    b. Make a **P** where Japan is.

    c. Make a **B** where China is.

    d. Make a **K** where Turkey is.

    e. Make an **L** where Italy is.

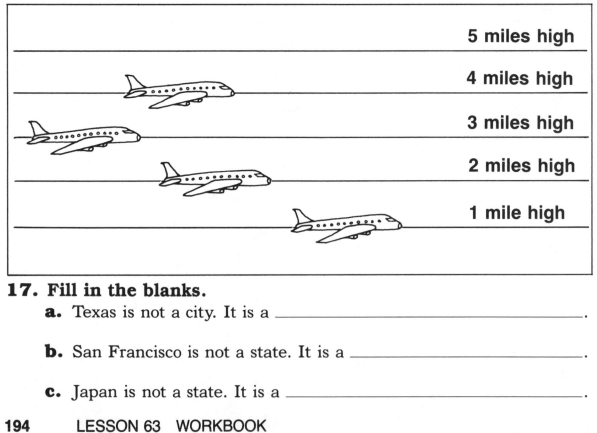

AFRICA

16. Make a box around the plane in the picture that is in the coldest air.

5 miles high

4 miles high

3 miles high

2 miles high

1 mile high

17. Fill in the blanks.

    a. Texas is not a city. It is a _____.

    b. San Francisco is not a state. It is a _____.

    c. Japan is not a state. It is a _____.

LESSON 64

A

Story items

1. **Finish the sentence.** Linda and Kathy were on a ship that was

   going from the United States to _____.

2. Did Linda and Kathy go in one of the lifeboats when the ship sank?

   _____

3. What will the girls use for a lifeboat? _____

4. Could Kathy swim well? _____

5. Could Linda swim well? _____

6. Here's a picture of Kathy and Linda on their crate.
   a. Draw a solid arrow on Linda's hand to show which way it is moving.
   b. Draw a dotted arrow on the crate to show which way it is moving.

7. The ship in the picture is sinking. It is making currents as it sinks. There's an arrow on one lifeboat to show which way the currents are pulling it. **Make an arrow** on each of the other objects to show which way it is being pulled.

Review items

8. a. Name a state in the United States that is bigger than Italy. _____

   b. Finish the sentence. Italy is shaped something like a _____.

9. Some people in the picture are holding sticks that are 1 meter long. Write **1 meter** under each stick that is 1 meter long.

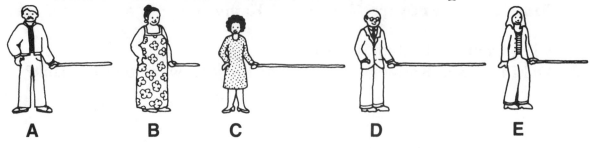

A   B   C   D   E

10. When are lifeboats used? _____

_____

11. Finish each sentence.

   a. The biggest state in the United States is _____.

   b. The second-biggest state in the United States is _____.

   c. The third-biggest state in the United States is _____.

12. Look at the map below.

   • Things that are this far apart on the map ⟵⟶ are 10 miles apart.

   • Things that are this far apart ⟵——⟶ are 20 miles apart.

   a. Write **10** in the circle if the line stands for 10 miles.

   b. Write **20** in the circle if the line stands for 20 miles.

   c. How far is it from the hill to the park? _____

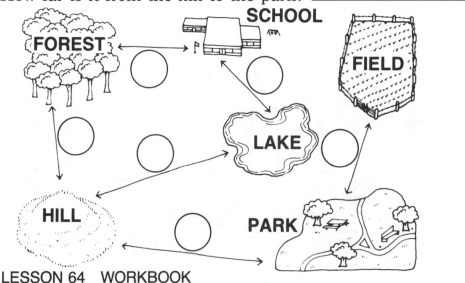

13. Look at the picture below.

    a. The food that three of the animals eat each day weighs as much as those animals. **Underline** those animals.

    b. The food that three of the animals eat each day does not weigh as much as those animals. **Cross out** those animals.

14. **Finish the sentence.** When we weigh very small things, we use

_____.

15. Look at the lines in the box below.

    a. Write **2** on each line that is 2 centimeters long.

    b. Write **3** on each line that is 3 centimeters long.

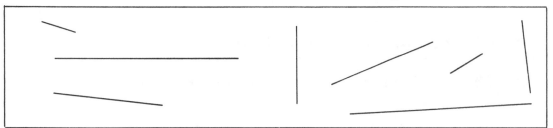

16. Look at the map.

    a. Write **north, south, east,** and **west** in the right boxes.

    b. Make a **J** where Japan is.

    c. Make a **C** where China is.

    d. Make a **T** where Turkey is.

    e. Make an **I** where Italy is.

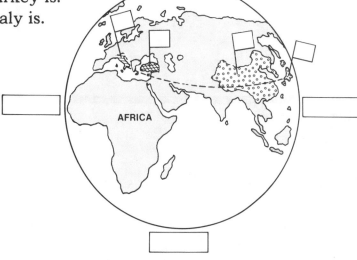

LESSON 65

A

In today's lesson, you read about ocean water. Use what you learned to do these items.

1. The picture below shows jars of water on a very cold day.

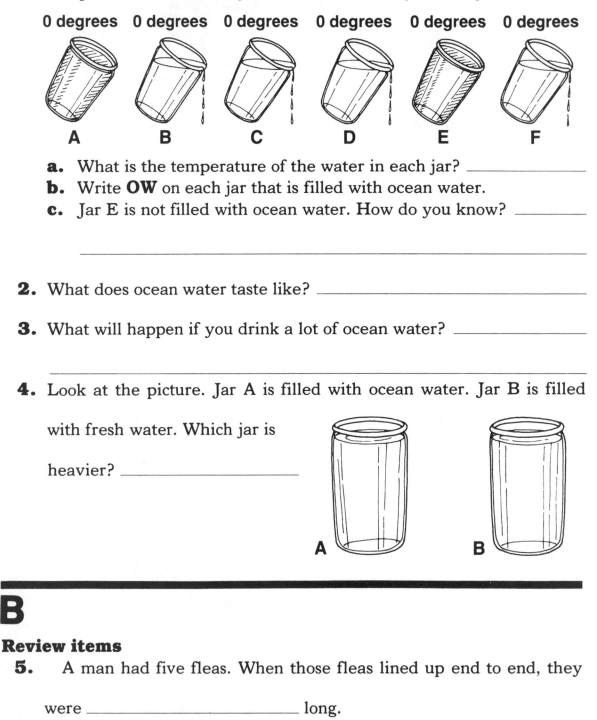

0 degrees 0 degrees 0 degrees 0 degrees 0 degrees 0 degrees

A   B   C   D   E   F

   a. What is the temperature of the water in each jar? _____

   b. Write **OW** on each jar that is filled with ocean water.

   c. Jar E is not filled with ocean water. How do you know? _____

_____

2. What does ocean water taste like? _____

3. What will happen if you drink a lot of ocean water? _____

_____

4. Look at the picture. Jar A is filled with ocean water. Jar B is filled

with fresh water. Which jar is

heavier? _____

A   B

B

Review items

   5. A man had five fleas. When those fleas lined up end to end, they

were _____ long.

The man had a pencil. It was a short pencil. So it weighed _____.

The man had three dogs. Two of them were the same size. They were a poodle and a pointer. They were _____ long. The third dog the man had looked something like a pointer, but it was shorter. It was brown and white and black. That dog could have been a _____ .

The man liked to go places. He ran a lot and he was very fast. He could run _____ .

The man liked to run with his dogs. His pointer was very fast. It could run _____ .

The man liked to fly in airplanes. He loved jets because they can fly at the speed of _____ .

These jets are so fast that they can fly from New York City to San Francisco in _____ hours. The flight from New York City to San Francisco is _____ miles.

6. Draw an arrow at A and an arrow at B to show which way the string will move when the toad moves the blue fly.

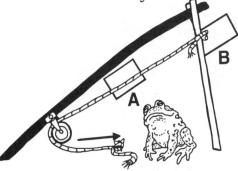

7. The ship in the picture is sinking. It is making currents as it sinks. **Make an arrow** on each object to show which way it is being pulled.

8. a. Finish the sentence. The land parts of the world are divided

into _____ .

b. What country do you live in? _____

9. a. Circle the ruler that will make the highest sound.

b. Underline the ruler that will make the lowest sound.

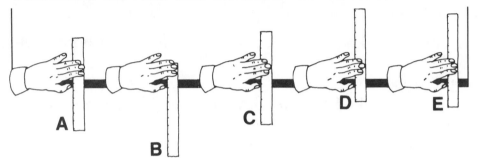

10. a. Does a dog weigh **more than a gram** or **less than a gram?**

_____

b. Does an ant weigh **more than a gram** or **less than a gram?**

_____

11. a. When a boy jumps this way ↖, there is a push against the

ground. Draw an arrow to show the direction of that push. _____

b. If a girl dove into a pool in this direction ↗, there would be a
push against the side of the pool. Draw an arrow to show the

direction of that push. _____

12. Look at the picture. It tells how many degrees each object is.

a. Which object is the hottest? _____

b. What is the temperature of that object? _____

c. Which object is the coldest? _____

d. What is the temperature of that object? _____

60 degrees   **30 degrees**   **90 degrees**

13. Fill in the blanks.

Liz liked cool weather. It was the middle of summer, and she wanted to go to a city that was cool in the summer. So she went to

the city of _____.

Liz knew that the temperature of an object tells how _____ that object is. When she left New York City, the air on the ground was 30 degrees. But when the plane went higher and higher, the air

outside the plane got _____.
When the plane was 6 miles high, the air outside the plane was

below zero. It was _____.
When the plane went from New York City to San Francisco, it was

going in which direction? _____.
The plane was facing the wind, so the name of the wind was a

_____.
Did the plane go **faster** or **slower** than a plane going in the

opposite direction? _____.
The air that rushed from the jet engines was going to the east, so

the jet engines moved toward the _____.
The jet engines were attached to parts of the plane. Those parts were

the _____.
As Liz flew along, she wanted to get a good look at things on the ground below. So she looked through something that makes things

look very big. She looked through _____.
She saw the city of Chicago. That city was between Denver and

_____.

14. Fill in the blanks.

a. Japan is not a state. It is a _____.

b. San Francisco is not a state. It is a _____.

c. Texas is not a city. It is a _____.

15. Each speedometer in the picture shows how fast the taxi is moving.

   a. How fast is taxi **A** going? _____

   b. How fast is taxi **B** going? _____

   c. Which taxi is going faster? _____

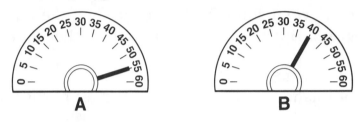

16. Figure out how tall each animal in the picture is. You know how tall one of the animals is.

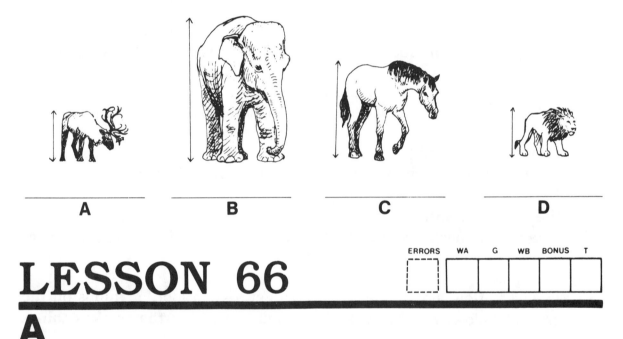

           A   B   C   D

LESSON 66

ERRORS	WA	G	WB	BONUS	T

A

In today's lesson, you read about islands. Use what you learned to do these items.

  1. a. There are three islands on the map. **Cross out** each island.

      b. **B** is not an island. Tell why.

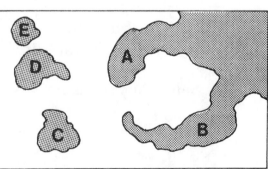

_____

_____

_____

B

Story items

2. Why did Linda have a hard time swimming to the crate? _____

_____

3. What did Linda and Kathy use for a lifeboat? _____

4. What did the girls use for paddles? _____

5. What made Linda's feet sore? _____

6. What would happen if you drank lots of ocean water? _____

_____

7. Something made sounds that told Linda they were near the shore.

What made those sounds? _____

8. As the girls walked along the beach, they could hardly see where

they were going. Tell why. _____

Review items

9. a. Finish the sentence. The temperature of an object tells how

_____ that object is.

b. Finish the rule about temperature. When an object gets

hotter, the temperature goes _____.

c. When a room gets hotter, which way does the temperature of the

room go? _____

d. A pan gets colder. So what do you know about the temperature

of the pan? _____

10. Look at the picture.

    a. Write **north, south, east,** and **west** in the right boxes.

    b. Which animal is facing into the wind? _____

    c. Which direction is that animal facing? _____

    d. So what's the name of the wind? _____

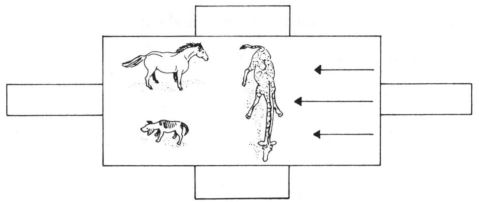

11. Some of the things in the picture below are insects and some are spiders.

    a. **Circle** the spiders.

    b. Object C is not a spider. Tell why. _____

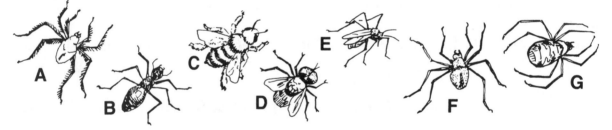

12. The picture below shows jars of water on a very cold day.

    a. What is the temperature of the water in each jar? _____

    b. Write **OW** on each jar that is filled with ocean water.

    c. Jar D is not filled with ocean water. How do you know?

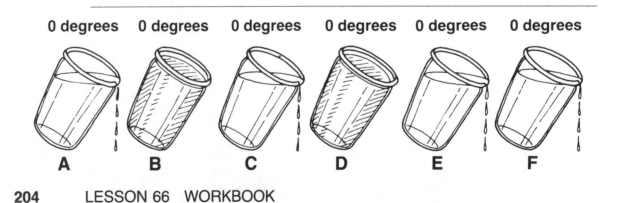

0 degrees   0 degrees   0 degrees   0 degrees   0 degrees   0 degrees

A   B   C   D   E   F

13. Look at the picture below. Jar **Y** is filled with ocean water. Jar **X** is filled with fresh water. Which jar is heavier? _____

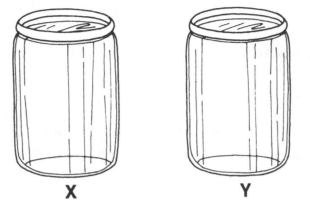

X   Y

14. Fill in the blank. The _____ inside a car tells how fast the car is moving.

15. What does ocean water taste like? _____

16. Some things in the picture weigh 1 gram. Some weigh 2 grams. Some weigh 5 grams. Fill in the blanks to tell how much each object weighs.

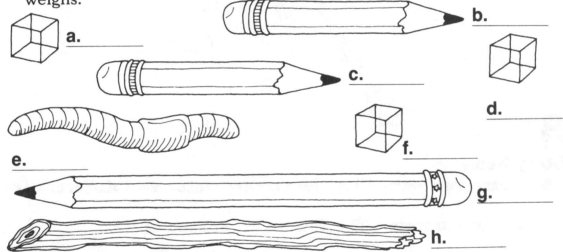

a. _____   b. _____

c. _____

d. _____

e. _____   f.

g. _____

h. _____

17. a. Finish the sentence. The land parts of the world are divided into _____ .

b. What country do you live in? _____

18. Fill in the blanks.

a. The United States is not a city. It is a _____ .

b. San Francisco is not a state. It is a _____ .

c. Denver is not a state. It is a _____ .

LESSON 67

A In today's lesson, you read about palm trees. Use what you learned to do these items.

1. Finish the sentence. Palm trees cannot live in places that get

_____.

2. What are the branches of palm trees called? _____

3. Name two things that grow on different palm trees.

① _____   ② _____

4. The picture below shows a coconut tree. On each line, write the name of the part.

a. _____

b. _____

c. _____

d. _____

B

Story items

5. Name two ways that the stream water was different from the ocean water. The water in the stream was _____

and _____.

6. A strange sound woke Linda in the morning. What was making that

strange sound? _____

7. Whose footprints did Linda and Kathy find on the beach? _____

8. Finish the sentence with words from the story. Linda said, "We have been walking in a circle. That means we are on

_____."

9. Did Linda and Kathy see anyone else when they were walking? _____

10. The map shows the island that Linda and Kathy were on.
    a. Write **north, south, east,** and **west** in the right boxes.
    b. **Draw a dotted line** to show where Linda and Kathy walked.
    c. **Make an X** to show where Linda was when she saw footprints.

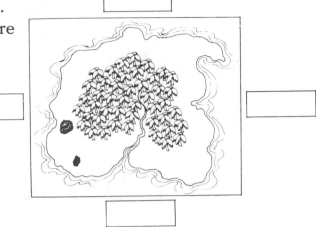

Review items

11. Look at the picture below.
    a. Make an arrow over each canoe to show which way the canoe is moving.
    b. Make an arrow under each paddle to show which way the paddle is moving in the water.

12. Look at the picture.
    a. Write **north, south, east,** and **west** in the right boxes.

    b. Which animal is facing into the wind? _____

    c. Which direction is that animal facing? _____

    d. So what's the name of the wind? _____

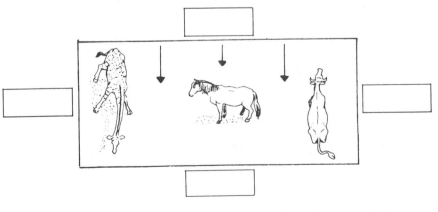

13. a. Some of the things in the picture below are insects, and some are spiders. **Underline** the spiders.

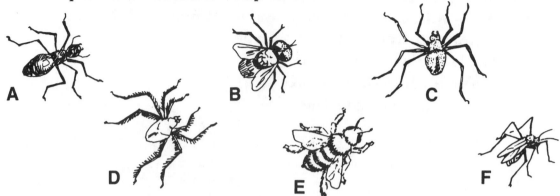

b. Object F is not a spider. Tell why. _____

14. a. Finish the sentence. The temperature of an object tells how

_____ that object is.

b. Finish the rule. When an object gets hotter, the temperature

goes _____.

15. Make an **I** on each island in the picture.

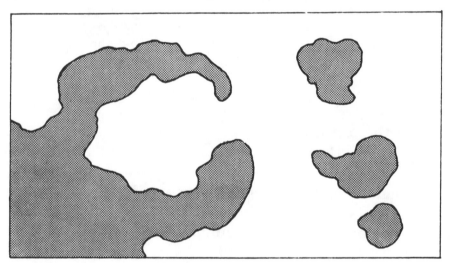

16. a. Let's say you are outside when the temperature is 20 degrees.

What is the temperature inside your body? _____

b. Let's say a fly is outside when the temperature is 20 degrees.

What is the temperature inside the fly's body? _____

17. In what direction do you fly to get from Italy to New York City? ____

18. Where are the gas tanks on a big jet? _____

LESSON 68

A

In today's lesson, you read about coconuts. Use what you learned to do these items.

1. How many shells does a coconut have? _____

2. a. Is it easy to break open a coconut? _____

    b. Tell why. _____

3. What is the juice inside a coconut called? _____

4. The picture below shows a coconut that is cut in half. On each line, write the name of the part.

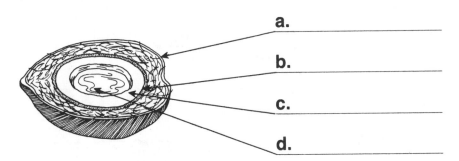

    a. _____

    b. _____

    c. _____

    d. _____

Story items

5. What was wrong with the first coconuts that the girls found? _____

_____

6. When Kathy shook the coconut, it sounded like a bottle that had water in it. What made the sound like water? _____

7. What did Linda and Kathy use to open the coconut? _____

8. Why did the girls want to make the monkeys mad? _____

_____

9. The picture shows a coconut.
    a. Make an **X** on the part that the girls ate.
    b. Make a **Y** on the part that the girls drank.

10. The picture below shows a coconut tree. On each line, write the name of the part.

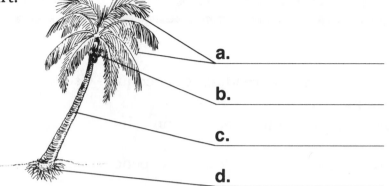

a. _____

b. _____

c. _____

d. _____

Review items

11. Some things in the picture weigh 1 gram. Some weigh 2 grams. Some weigh 5 grams. Fill in the blanks to tell how much each object weighs.

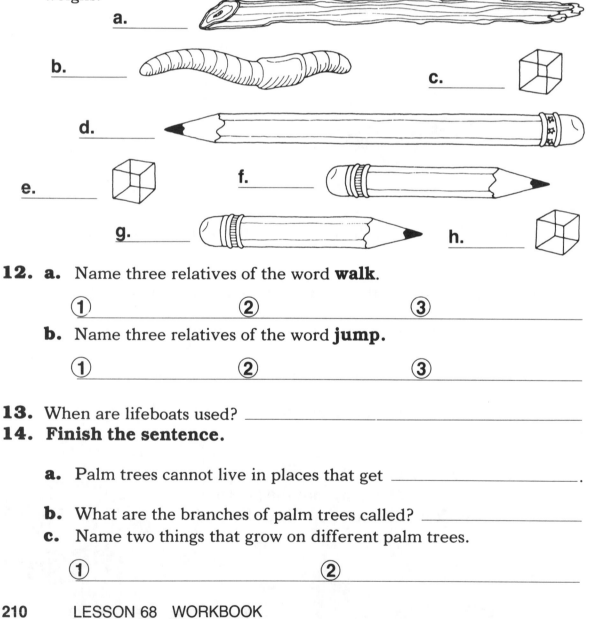

a. _____

b. _____

c. _____

d. _____

e. _____

f. _____

g. _____

h. _____

12. a. Name three relatives of the word **walk**.

① _____ ② _____ ③ _____

b. Name three relatives of the word **jump**.

① _____ ② _____ ③ _____

13. When are lifeboats used? _____

14. Finish the sentence.

a. Palm trees cannot live in places that get _____ .

b. What are the branches of palm trees called? _____

c. Name two things that grow on different palm trees.

① _____ ② _____

15. Look at the map below.
    a. Write **north, south, east,** and **west** in the right boxes.
    b. Make an **X** where Italy is.
    c. Make an **A** where New York City is.

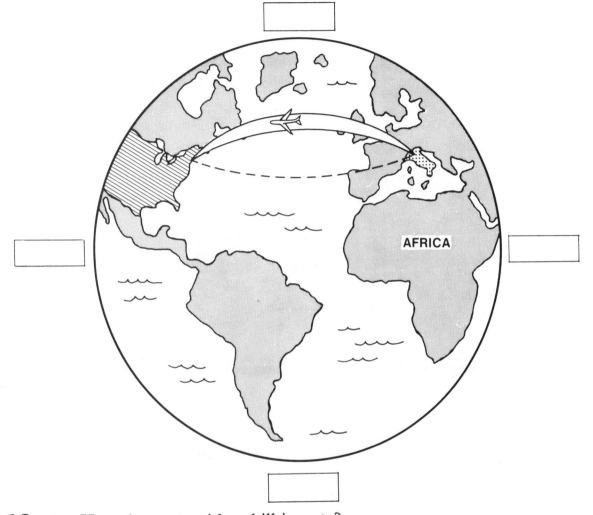

16. a. How do most spiders kill insects? _____
    b. **Finish the sentence.** When a spider wraps an insect in a web,

    the insect looks like a _____.

17. Write **warm-blooded** after each animal that is warm-blooded.

    a. man _____

    b. dog _____

    c. ant _____

    d. horse _____

    e. butterfly _____

LESSON 69

A

In today's lesson, you read about water wheels. Use what you learned to do these items.

1. Look at the picture of a water wheel.
   a. **Draw an arrow** from the **X** to show which way the blade will move.
   b. **Draw a circular arrow** around the end of the shaft to show which way the shaft will move.

B

Story items

2. What was the only thing Linda and Kathy ate for two days? _____

3. Why did Linda and Kathy want to catch some fish? _____

_____

4. What did they use for fishhooks? _____

5. What did they use for a fishing line? _____

6. Were there many fish in the water? _____

7. Did Linda and Kathy catch many fish with their hooks and lines? ____

8. The girls made hooks and lines to catch fish. Then they made something else to catch fish.
   a. What else did they make? _____

   b. What did they make it out of? _____

9. What happened when the girls tried to pull the fishing net out of the

water? _____

Review items

10. When are lifeboats used? _____

11. **a.** Name three relatives of the word **run.**

     ①_____ ②_____ ③_____

  b. Name three relatives of the word **sit.**

     ①_____ ②_____ ③_____

12. Write **warm-blooded** after each animal that is warm-blooded.

  a. spider _____

  b. woman _____

  c. cow _____

  d. fly _____

  e. cat _____

13. **a.** How many shells do coconuts have? _____

  b. Is it easy to break open a coconut? _____

  c. Tell why. _____

  d. What is the juice inside a coconut called? _____

14. The picture below shows a coconut that is cut in half. On each line, write the name of the part.

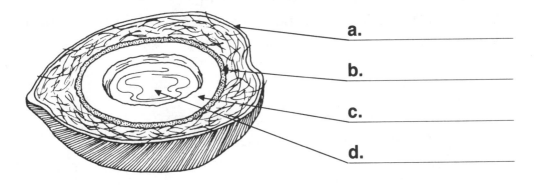

  a. _____

  b. _____

  c. _____

  d. _____

15. Name a state in the United States that is bigger than Japan. _____

16. The dotted arrow shows which way the girl will jump. Make a solid arrow on the back of the boat to show which way it will move.

17. a. Does a water strider weigh **more than a gram** or **less than a gram?** _____

b. Does a hamburger weigh **more than a gram** or **less than a gram?** _____

LESSON 70

ERRORS	WA	G	CO	WB	BONUS	T

A In today's lesson, you read about pounds. Use what you learned to do these items.

1. Fill in the blanks.

   a. My name is _____ .

   b. I weigh _____ .

2. About how much does your storybook weigh? _____

B Story items

3. Look at the picture.

   a. Write **north, south, east,** and **west** in the right boxes.
   b. Write **noon** on the sun you see at noon.
   c. Write **early morning** on the sun you see early in the morning.
   d. Write **evening** on the sun you see in the evening.

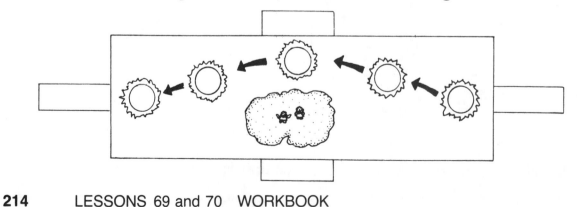

4. This map does not have north at the top. You have to figure out where north is.

    a. Look at the arrows. Write **1** on the first sun the girls see in the morning.

    b. Write the direction in the box next to sun **1**.

    c. Write **3** on the sun the girls see at noon.

    d. Write **5** on the last sun they see at the end of the day.

    e. Write the direction in the box next to sun **5**.

    f. Now turn the map so that **north** is on the top. Fill in the other boxes.

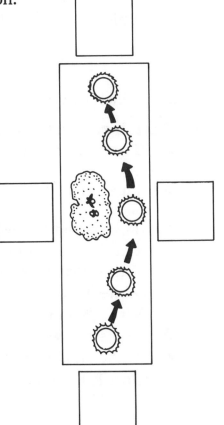

Review items

5. The picture shows a water wheel. The arrow shows which way the water is falling.

    a. Draw an arrow to show which way the blade will move.

    b. Draw a circular arrow around the end of the shaft to show which way the shaft will move.

6. Finish each sentence.

    a. The biggest state in the United States is _____.

    b. The second-biggest state in the United States is _____.

    c. The third-biggest state in the United States is _____.

7. a. Which eye works like one drop, a human's eye or a fly's eye?

_____

    b. Which eye works like many drops? _____

8. Finish each sentence.

    a. The United States is a _____.

    b. Japan is a _____.

    c. The United States is made up of fifty _____.

9. Look at the map below.

    a. Write **north, south, east,** and **west** in the right boxes.

    b. Write **M** where New York City is.

    c. Write **K** where San Francisco is.

    d. Make a **B** where Japan is.

    e. Make an **O** where the Pacific Ocean is.

10. a. In each picture below, draw a circle around every plane that will go the fastest.

b. Draw an arrow on the cloud in each picture to show which way it is moving.

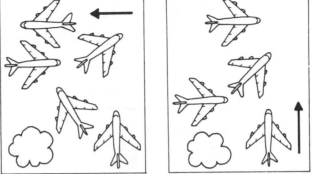

11. a. Name three cities you might fly over if you flew from New York City to San Francisco.

①_____ ②_____ ③_____

b. How far is it from New York City to San Francisco?

_____

c. How long does that trip take on a jet? _____

d. Does it take **more time** or **less time** to fly from San Francisco

to New York City? _____

12. For each item, tell if the temperature went up or the temperature went down.

a. The room went from 70 degrees to 40 degrees. What happened

to the temperature? _____

b. The water went from 30 degrees to 80 degrees. What happened

to the temperature? _____

13. Finish the rule. When something moves in one direction, _____

_____.

14. a. Circle the youngest fly.

b. Underline the oldest fly.

A   B   C   D

15. Look at the lines in the box below.
   a. Write **1** on each line that is 1 centimeter long.
   b. Write **2** on each line that is 2 centimeters long.

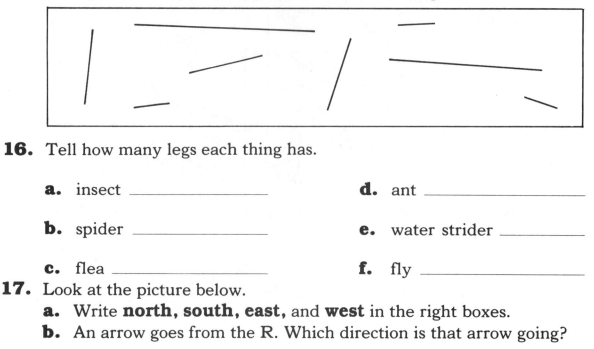

16. Tell how many legs each thing has.

   a. insect _____

   b. spider _____

   c. flea _____

   d. ant _____

   e. water strider _____

   f. fly _____

17. Look at the picture below.
   a. Write **north, south, east,** and **west** in the right boxes.
   b. An arrow goes from the R. Which direction is that arrow going?

   _____

   c. Make an arrow that goes north from the J.
   d. Draw the smoke in the picture.

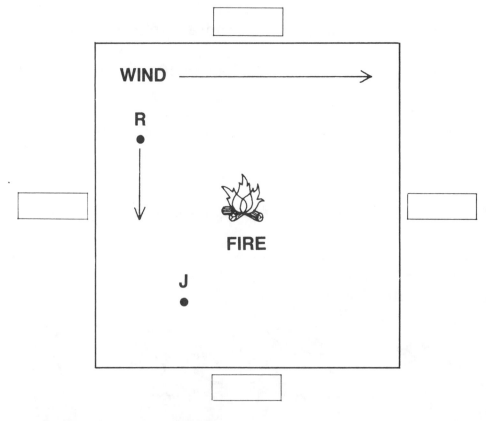

Appendix A
FACT GAMES 1-7

SCORECARD

X̶1̶	X̶2̶	3	X̶4̶	5	6	7	8	9	10
11	12	13	14	15	16	17	18	19	20
21	22	23	24	25	26	27	28	29	30

FG	BONUS	TOTAL

Fact game 1

(after lesson 10)

1. As you touch each tree, tell if it grew in a forest or in a field.

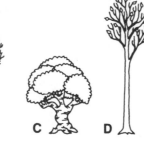

A   B   C   D

2. As you touch each letter, name the part.

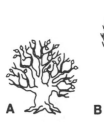

3. a. Which arrow shows the direction the canoe is moving — A or B?

  b. Which arrow shows the direction the paddle is moving — C or D?

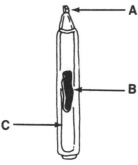

4. As you touch each letter, name the place.

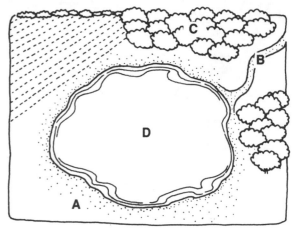

5. a. Which canoe is moving very fast?

  b. Which canoe is not moving at all?

6. Name two kinds of canoes that Indians made.

SCORECARD

1	2	3	4	5	6	7	8	9	10
11	12	13	14	15	16	17	18	19	20
21	22	23	24	25	26	27	28	29	30

FG	BONUS	TOTAL

Fact game 2
(after lesson 20)

2. As you touch each person, tell what kind of diet the person should be on: **a diet to lose weight, a diet to put on weight,** or **a diet to stay healthy.**

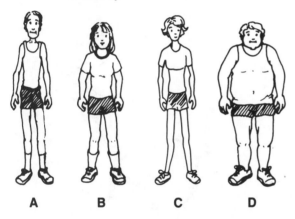

A   B   C   D

3. a. Where do the fleas in flea circuses come from?

   b. What's the first thing they must be taught?

4. As you touch each dog, name the kind of dog.

5. How many centimeters are in one meter?

6. As you touch each object, tell if it is **one meter long** or **two meters long.**

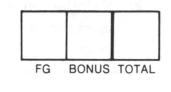

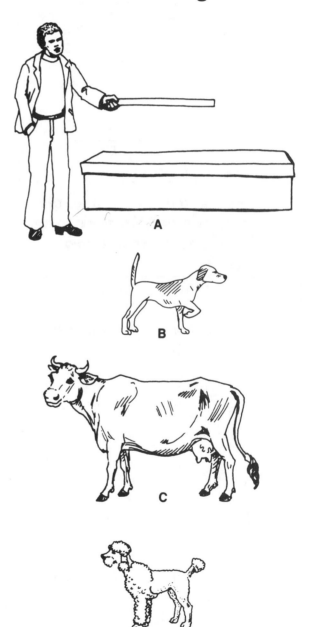

7. Tell the letters for all the lines that are one centimeter long.

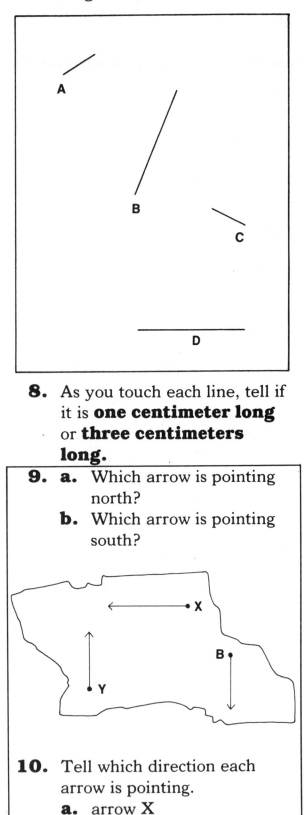

8. As you touch each line, tell if it is **one centimeter long** or **three centimeters long.**

9. a. Which arrow is pointing north?

    b. Which arrow is pointing south?

10. Tell which direction each arrow is pointing.

    a. arrow X

    b. arrow Y

11. Tell how many legs each animal has.

    a. insect

    b. spider

    c. reindeer

12. Tell the letters for all the reindeer.

SCORECARD

1	2	3	4	5	6	7	8	9	10
11	12	13	14	15	16	17	18	19	20
21	22	23	24	25	26	27	28	29	30

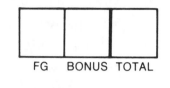

FG   BONUS   TOTAL

Fact game 3

(after lesson 30)

2. Tell the letters of the animals
that live on the land.

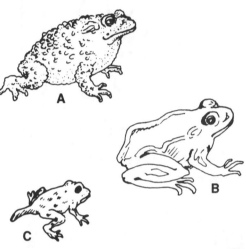

3. Which arrow shows

a. the way the air will leave
the jet engine — A
or B?

b. the way the plane will
move — C or D?

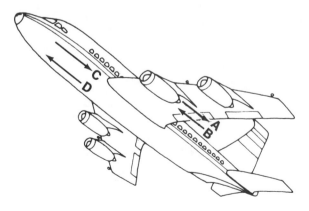

4. Which circle would you see
a. through binoculars?
b. without binoculars?

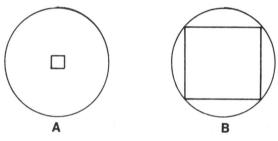

5. Which balloon lets
a. the most light come
through?
b. the least light come
through?

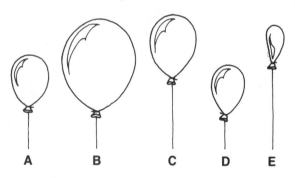

6. Which arrow shows
a. the way the air will leave
Goad — A or B?
b. the way Goad will
move — C or D?

7. Which arrow shows
   a. the way the air will leave the balloon — A or B?
   b. the way the balloon will move — C or D?

8. a. Show how long a centimeter is.
   b. Show how long a meter is.

9. Touch each balloon. Tell which solid arrow shows the way the balloon will move.

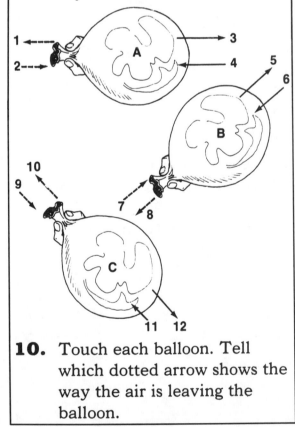

10. Touch each balloon. Tell which dotted arrow shows the way the air is leaving the balloon.

11. The arrow shows which way the wind is blowing. Which smoke is blowing the right way?

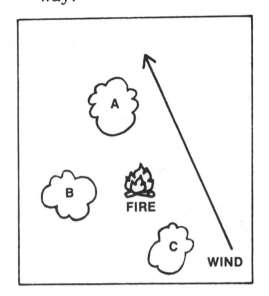

12. Tell the letters of the toads in the picture.

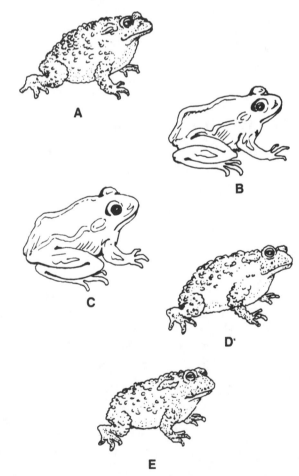

SCORECARD

1	2	3	4	5	6	7	8	9	10
11	12	13	14	15	16	17	18	19	20
21	22	23	24	25	26	27	28	29	30

FG	BONUS	TOTAL

Fact game 4
(after lesson 40)

2. Which grow up faster
   a. boys or girls?
   b. dogs or mice?
3. a. How many ants weigh as much as a peanut?
   b. If an ant weighed as much as a dog, it could carry an object that weighs as much as

_____.

4. a. Show how long a meter is.
   b. Show how long a centimeter is.
5. Which ruler will make
   a. the highest sound?
   b. the lowest sound?

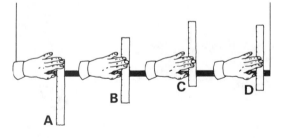

6. As you touch each object, tell if it weighs **less than a gram, one gram,** or **five grams.**

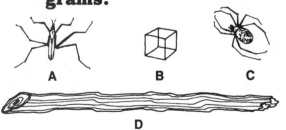

7. As you touch each letter, name the place.

8. a. What are the land parts of the world divided into?
   b. What country do you live in?
9. a. What is the world called?
   b. What is most of the world covered with?
10. a. What is dew?
   b. When does dew form?
11. As you touch each animal, tell what happened to the animal when it fell from a cliff.
   • **wasn't hurt**
   • **was hurt**
   • **was killed**

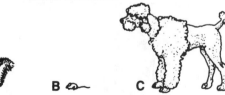

12. When Nancy became very small, she changed in other ways too. Name two ways she changed.

SCORECARD

1	2	3	4	5	6	7	8	9	10
11	12	13	14	15	16	17	18	19	20
21	22	23	24	25	26	27	28	29	30

FG	BONUS	TOTAL

Fact game 5
(after lesson 50)

2. Which picture shows Herman when the cab is

   a. standing still?

   b. going 50 miles per hour?

3. **a.** When flies are born, they are worms called

     _____.

   b. Where do flies change size — **on the inside** or **on the outside?**

4. The dotted arrows show which way the people will jump. Which arrows show the way the objects will move?

5. As you touch each line, tell if it stands for **12 hundred miles** or **25 hundred miles.**

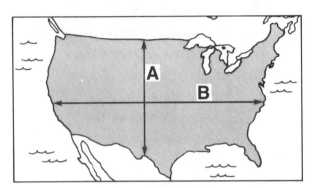

6. **a.** How fast is the fastest turtle going?

   b. How fast is the fastest girl going?

2

10

1

14

7. As you touch each letter, tell the name of the city.

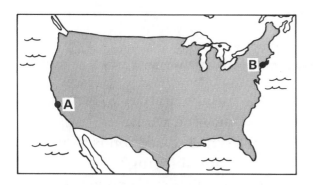

8. a. Tell the temperature of the hottest object.

   b. Tell the temperature of the coldest object.

40 degrees   **80 degrees**   **60 degrees**

9. About how many meters are in one mile?

10. Tell how fast each object can go.

   a. a jet plane

   b. a pointer

   c. a racing car

11. As you touch each speedometer, tell how fast the car is moving.

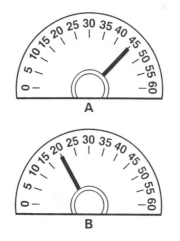

12. When something moves in one direction, _____ .

SCORECARD

1	2	3	4	5	6	7	8	9	10
11	12	13	14	15	16	17	18	19	20
21	22	23	24	25	26	27	28	29	30

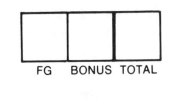

FG   BONUS   TOTAL

Fact game 6
(after lesson 60)

2. Where are the gas tanks on a big jet?

3. As you touch each animal, tell if it is **cold-blooded** or **warm-blooded.**

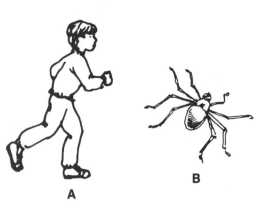

A

B

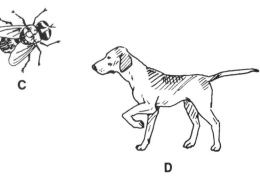

C

D

4. a. The United States is made up of fifty

_____ .

b. The biggest state in the United States is

_____ .

c. The second-biggest state in the United States is

_____ .

5. a. Which animal is facing into the wind?

b. Which direction is that animal facing?

c. So what's the name of the wind?

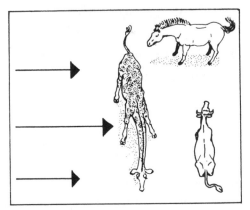

6. When the temperature is 8 degrees, what's the temperature

a. inside your body?

b. inside a fly's body?

7. As you touch each letter, tell the name of the place.

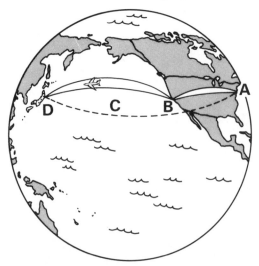

8. As you touch each letter, name the country.

9. Tell the direction you fly to go
  a. from Italy to New York City.
  b. from San Francisco to Japan.
10. a. How far is it from New York City to San Francisco?
  b. How long does that trip take on a jet?

11. As you touch each letter, name the city.
12. a. Tell the number of the plane that is going faster.
  b. Why is it going faster?

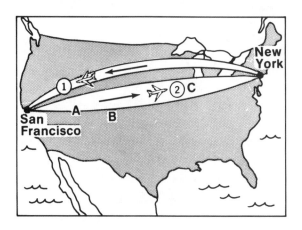

SCORECARD

1	2	3	4	5	6	7	8	9	10
11	12	13	14	15	16	17	18	19	20
21	22	23	24	25	26	27	28	29	30

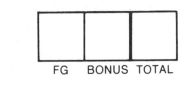

FG   BONUS   TOTAL

Fact game 7
(after lesson 70)

2. As you touch each letter, name the part.

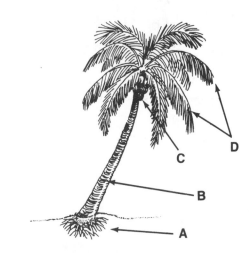

3. Tell the letters that show islands.

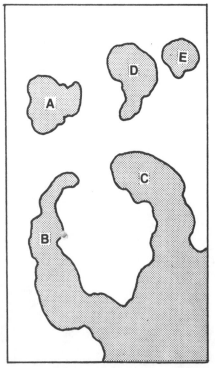

4. a. Which jar is filled with ocean water?

b. What does ocean water taste like?

c. What will happen if you drink lots of ocean water?

0 degrees   0 degrees

A   B

5. a. Read all the words in the **walk** family.

b. Read all the words in the **run** family.

jump	running	sat
book	rider	ran
eats	walks	walked
walker	runner	talking

6. As you touch each jar, tell the temperature of the water in that jar.

20 degrees   40 degrees   15 degrees

A   B   C

7. Tell about how much your storybook weighs.

8. Tell the letter of the sun you see
   a. at noon
   b. early in the morning
   c. in the evening

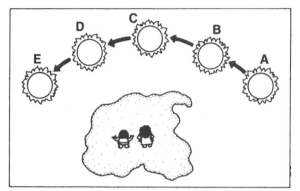

9. a. Which arrow shows the way the blade will move?
   b. Which circular arrow shows the way the shaft will move?

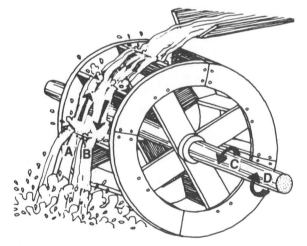

10. Which weighs more, **a cup of ocean water** or **a cup of fresh water?**

11. As you touch each letter, name the part.

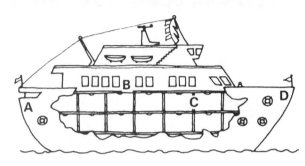

12. As you touch each letter, name the part.

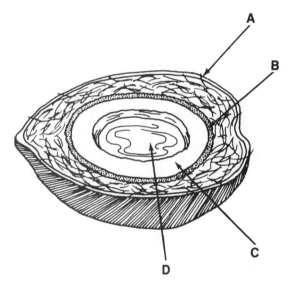

Appendix B
FACT GAMES 1-7
ANSWER KEY

Fact game 1

1. A—field
   B—forest
   C—field
   D—forest

2. A—felt tip
   B—ink
   C—shaft

3. **a.** A
   b. D

4. A—shore
   B—path
   C—forest
   D—middle of the lake

5. **a.** A
   b. B

6. dugout canoes, bark canoes

Fact game 2

2. A—diet to put on weight
   B—diet to stay healthy
   C—diet to put on weight
   D—diet to lose weight

3. **a.** Russia
   b. to walk

4. A—pointer
   B—beagle
   C—poodle

5. 1 hundred

6. A—2 meters long
   B—1 meter long
   C—2 meters long
   D—1 meter long

7. A, C

8. A—1 centimeter long
   B—3 centimeters long
   C—1 centimeter long
   D—3 centimeters long

9. **a.** Y
   b. B

10. **a.** west
    b. north

11. **a.** 6
    b. 8
    c. 4

12. A, D

Fact game 3

2. A, B

3. a. A
   b. D

4. a. B
   b. A

5. a. B
   b. E

6. a. B
   b. C

7. a. A
   b. C

8. a. *Player holds up fingers to show a centimeter.*
   b. *Player holds up arms to show a meter.*

9. Balloon A—3
   Balloon B—5
   Balloon C—12

10. Balloon A—1
   Balloon B—8
   Balloon C—10

11. A

12. A, D, E

Fact game 4

2. a. girls
   b. mice

3. a. 1 hundred
   b. 10 dogs

4. a. *Player holds up arms to show a meter.*
   b. *Player holds up fingers to show a centimeter.*

5. a. C
   b. A

6. A—less than a gram
   B—1 gram
   C—less than a gram
   D—5 grams

7. A—South America
   B—United States
   C—Mexico
   D—Canada

8. a. countries
   b. *Ask your teacher for the answer.*

9. a. earth
   b. water

10. a. little drops of water
   b. at night; when the air gets cooler

11. A—was hurt
   B—wasn't hurt
   C—was killed

12. *Player names two:* Her voice got higher; she didn't get hurt when she fell from high places; it was hard to drink through the skin on water; every day, she ate about as much as she weighed.

Fact game 5

2. **a.** A
   b. B

3. **a.** maggots
   b. on the inside

4. A, D

5. A—12 hundred miles
   B—25 hundred miles

6. **a.** 2 miles per hour
   b. 14 miles per hour

7. A—San Francisco
   B—New York City

8. **a.** 80 degrees
   b. 40 degrees

9. 16 hundred

10. **a.** 5 hundred miles
    b. 35 miles per hour
    c. 2 hundred miles per hour

11. **a.** 45 miles per hour
    b. 20 miles per hour

12. there's a push in the
    opposite direction

Fact game 6

2. in the wings

3. A—warm-blooded
   B—cold-blooded
   C—cold-blooded
   D—warm-blooded

4. **a.** states
   b. Alaska
   c. Texas

5. **a.** horse
   b. west
   c. west wind

6. **a.** 37 degrees
   b. 8 degrees

7. A—New York City
   B—San Francisco
   C—Pacific Ocean
   D—Japan

8. A—Italy
   B—Turkey
   C—China

9. **a.** west
   b. west

10. **a.** 25 hundred miles
    b. 6 hours

11. A—Salt Lake City
    B—Denver
    C—Chicago

12. **a.** 2
    b. Because it's
    going in the same
    direction as the
    wind.

Fact game 7

2. A—roots
   B—trunk
   C—coconuts
   D—fronds

3. A, D, E

4. **a.** A
   b. salt
   c. You'll get thirstier.

5. **a.** walker, walks, walked
   b. running, runner, ran

6. A—20 degrees
   B—40 degrees
   C—15 degrees

7. 1 pound

8. **a.** C
   b. A
   c. E

9. **a.** B
   b. C

10. a cup of ocean water

11. A—stern
    B—deck
    C—bulkhead
    D—prow

12. A—outer shell
    B—inner shell
    C—coconut meat
    D—coconut milk